MATTHEW'S STORY OF JESUS

COMPANION VOLUMES

Mark's Story of Jesus by Werner H. Kelber
Luke's Story of Jesus by O. C. Edwards, Jr.
John's Story of Jesus by Robert Kysar

MATTHEW'S STORY OF JESUS

Richard A. Edwards

FORTRESS PRESS   PHILADELPHIA

Library of Congress Cataloging in Publication Data

Edwards, Richard Alan.
  Matthew's story of Jesus.

  1. Bible. N.T. Matthew—Criticism, interpretation, etc. I. Title.
  BS2575.2.E38 1985   226'.2066   84–48711
  ISBN 0–8006–1619–7

1257H84   Printed in the United States of America   1–1619

For
June

Contents

Introduction

The Gospel of Matthew is a *story* of Jesus, a narrative, not an essay or chronicle. Since, as we will see, the various parts of this story are carefully interrelated, it is inappropriate and misleading to impose upon it a precise outline. At present there are two primary suggestions about the proper outline of the Gospel, both of which are based on repeated phrases or formulas. In contrast, the method used here will follow the development of the plot or the flow of the narrative. Rather than view the work as a completed or finished whole, I intend to examine the narrative from the point of view of a reader who begins at the beginning. This approach is less concerned with an outline and more interested in the way the narrator anticipates or recalls ideas or subjects in the progress of the story. The narrative will seem to double back at times as the narrator builds his impressions in the reader's mind. Since reading is a cumulative process that extends over a period of time, the sequence of information and its relation to earlier portions of the story will be my primary concern.

In my treatment, Matthew's story will be divided into sections, but they should not be considered complete, self-contained units. Rather, they are basic segments or moments in the continuing narration.

Matt. 1:1—4:22   Establishing the Framework
                   of the Story

Matt. 4:23—7:29   The Demands of the Kingdom

Matt. 8:1—11:1   The Power of the Kingdom

Matt. 11:2—18:35   The Response to the Coming
                   of the Kingdom

Matt. 19:1—25:46   The Message of the Kingdom
                   Presented in Judea

Matt. 26:1—28:20   The Conflict Takes Place

Typical of biblical narrative is an extensive use of direct speech. This is an especially prominent feature of Matthew. Of course, these speeches or discourses within Matthew have often been noted. But we must consider the effect on the reader. When a character is presented primarily by quotation, there is always an ambiguity that requires the reader to be more involved in the story. Instead of being told by the narrator what the individual is like, the reader is forced to make an independent evaluation. This reader participation produces, among other things, a growing sense of concern. Furthermore, because there is some ambiguity, it is important that the narrator establish the reliability (or its lack) of the speaker. Thus, the opening of a narrative is most significant in giving the reader a perspective from which to judge the characters.

Because the narrator of a story is important, especially in establishing a point of view, we must pay special attention to our narrator's "reticent-omniscient" point of view. There are only a few direct comments by the narrator in this story and yet the narrator moves around at will, has inside information about participants, and, at times, reveals the inner thoughts of some characters. Once the story begins, he or she stays very close to Jesus, hearing conversations and witnessing "closed" meetings. The result is that the reader is encouraged to accept the narrator's reliability. And, since the narrator is reliable, the reader also accepts the reliability of the narration. Therefore one of our tasks is to locate those features of the story that encourage the reader to make these judgments.

I must add a special comment about the terms "reader" and "narrator." Literary critics make a careful distinction between the narratee, the implied reader, and the real reader, and also between the narrator, implied author, and the real author. Using these terms, this study of Matthew is an analysis of the implied author's use of the narrator and the effect this has on the implied reader. I have chosen to use the simpler terms—"narrator" and "reader." Thus, I ask the reader of this volume to make that adjustment; when I speak about the reader I am not attempting to describe a real person (of the first, third, tenth, or twentieth century) but the person posited *by the text* as the reader.

Finally, this book is neither a commentary nor a retelling of the story but an attempt to point to significant features of the narration. Some details of the Gospel will not be mentioned—not because they can be overlooked but because it is not possible for me to be exhaustive here. Those items that affect the reader will be noted and their relation to the developing strategy of the narrator analyzed.

1
Establishing the Framework of the Story

1:1—4:22

OPENING (1:1–17)

Matthew's story begins in a traditional way, with a genealogy. It is a typical patriarchal listing. There are features in it, however, that attract a reader's attention.

The superscription (1:1) refers to Jesus as the Messiah (Christ) who is the son of both Abraham and David, thereby documenting the extent of his Jewish heritage. As yet, a reader has no idea what significance this has for the story. However, as the listing of males proceeds, a number of women are mentioned. The list of names is also interrupted by a reference to the deportation to Babylon (1:11–12), the only time in the genealogy when an event is reported; it breaks into the sequence of names even though the repetition of the genealogy remains intact. When the reader reaches the end of the listing, however, the entire sequence is broken: Joseph is called "the husband of Mary" rather than the father of Jesus. The reader's attention is caught by the words, "Mary, of whom Jesus was born" (1:16), not only because of the change in sequence but also because another woman is mentioned. For the moment, one cannot be sure of her significance. The genealogy ends with the phrase "Jesus who is called Christ." Just as the story opens with a reference to Jesus Christ, the genealogy ends with the title Christ (1:1, 16). The emphasis on Jesus' mother, partially anticipated by the mention of women earlier in the genealogy, is itself unusual enough to encourage the reader to expect some further explanation.

This expectation is partially satisfied in the summary statement of Matt. 1:17. Here we are informed that the time from Abraham to the Christ can be divided into three groups of fourteen generations each. The significance of the deportation is now clear—it is the exile itself and not Jechoniah that is important. The three names of 1:1 are now repeated in 1:17, with the addition of the very regular time pattern. But there is more implied in this verse. The very orderliness of the division implies that God has had a hand in this arrangement, that it is not mere circumstance or hindsight. God's involvement in the lives of Abraham and David is well known. Furthermore, in the prophetic tradition the exile is also interpreted as part of God's plan, albeit a punishment occasioned by human action. The narrator's intentions are put into a compact unit.

The reader, then, is introduced to the basic framework of this story of Jesus. His origins reach back along an extended lineage within which God has been active. The significance of Mary is yet to be explained but the reader is alerted to the reality of divine influence in this story.

BIRTH AND INFANCY (1:18—2:23)

The construction of this framework continues in the next episode, usually called "the Birth of Jesus." Since it is the narrator's intention to establish the authority and reliability of Jesus, in this episode we are given the reason for the enigmatic reference to Joseph, Mary's husband, who is *not* called Jesus' father (1:16). The narrator is not primarily interested in Jesus' birth. Rather, we have an incident that shows what it means to say that Joseph is a just or righteous man (1:19). Notice that the only direct discourse is the word of the "angel of the Lord" who speaks to Joseph in dreams. The narrator knows what Joseph thinks and what he experiences as he dreams. Note also that the narrator does not speak as Joseph; it is not autobiographical. Rather, the reader is encouraged to accept the narrator's reliability because the story is told from a favored point of view. Joseph is said to accept the message of the dream as a message from God; the "Birth of Jesus" episode is really a story about the way Joseph understands and accepts the divine origin of the child, Jesus.

The first of Matthew's fulfillment quotations appears in the midst of this incident (1:22). The introduction to these Old Testament (OT) quotations (see also 2:5, 15, 17, 23) is a peculiar feature of Matthew's Gospel. From a narrative perspective, it is interesting that this first fulfillment quotation interrupts the story and stands out as a comment from the narrator. By explicitly pointing out the precise continuity between the OT and these events, the narrator gives the reader a further reason to accept the validity of his comments while at the same time establishing the role of God in these events. The birth of the Christ is part of God's plan. Although the prophet is not named, the significance of the prophets and their reliability as representatives of God's will is a feature of the story that the narrator will continue to stress. What Joseph accepts is indeed God's work.

The quotation itself (from Isa. 7:14) predicts the virginal conception of the Messiah. He will be recognized as *Emmanuel* even though his given name is to be Jesus, as the angel commanded. It is especially significant that the narrator explains the word Emmanuel: "which means, God with us" (1:23). Many scholars have pointed out that this comment is echoed at the conclusion of the Gospel (28:16–20), when Jesus promises to be "with" his disciples until the end of the age. The dream and the quotation help to affirm the control God exercises throughout this narrative, and, in addition, the OT itself explicitly confirms what the narrator reports.

By the end of chap. 1, the reader is prepared to accept the truth of what is to follow. Jesus, the main character, born of a divine father, is a descendant of the great leaders of Israel. His birth comes at the culmination of a specific and organized plan. His stepfather accepts his divine origin because of the direct word of an angel. The inspired OT writings verify the control God has over these events.

It comes as no surprise, then, that Joseph obeys when he awakens; he is a just, righteous, obedient man. Only then does the narrator report Jesus' birth, in as simple and straightforward a way as possible.

The transition to the next episode (2:1) draws the reader's attention from a prebirth event to an incident after the birth, that is, to the wise men (2:1–23). We are informed in an offhand way where he was born, in Bethlehem, the first time that has been mentioned, and when, "in the days of Herod the King." The "behold" *(idou)* of 2:1 focuses the reader's attention on the main point—the arrival of the wise men.

The wise men are quoted as saying that they have come to worship a newborn king because of the appearance of his star. This sign in the heavens is a further instance of the divine guidance stressed in these opening chapters. The narrator reports that Herod and "all Jerusalem with him" are disturbed (2:3); God's action is greeted with less enthusiasm than expected. Herod, consulting with his religious leaders, is informed that Bethlehem is the site of the Messiah's birth, as foretold by the "prophet." The quotation speaks of a ruler of "my people Israel" (2:6).

The difficulty the reader expects, because of the narrator's comment about the city's reaction to the Magi, is confirmed when Herod summons them "secretly" (2:7) to get more detailed information. His hypocrisy is obvious when he says that he too wants to worship the Messiah. The narrator prepared us to recognize this duplicity by the earlier description of Herod: he is "troubled" and he acts "secretly."

The star guides the wise men to Bethlehem. The question they asked at Jerusalem and the information they received there were perhaps unnecessary for the completion of the trip, but not for the implementation of God's plan. They present gifts to Jesus and worship him. The ominous side of the situation emerges when the narrator mentions that they were warned in a dream not to return to Herod (2:12). Since we already know about the reliability and significance of dreams, no further details are needed; it is divine intervention. Our suspicions about Herod are confirmed and the Magi are seen to be obedient pagans.

The action moves quickly now. Joseph dreams again and is warned, specifically, about Herod's malicious intent (2:13). Thus the narrator verifies our suspicions about Herod's integrity by reporting the angel's words. Notice, however, that not even this act is fortuitous. The fulfillment quotation in 2:15 reminds the reader both of God's plan and also of Jesus' divine origins ("my Son"). This is the first time Jesus is specifically called Son of God.

The time-scheme at the beginning of the next episode (2:16) is slightly confused. We are told in 2:15 that the family stays in Egypt until Herod dies and then the quotation refers to the family being recalled to Judea. The narrator is anticipating later events and informing us of Jesus' continued safety.

After this flash-forward we return to Herod and Jerusalem (2:16–18). The narrator reports Herod's "furious rage" when he realizes he has been tricked by the Magi. This detail about Herod's motives and character reinforces the negative attitude already planted in the mind of the reader, especially when we learn that he intends to kill all male children in Bethlehem. Since, however, the next fulfillment quotation follows immediately (2:17), the reader knows that even this is part of God's plan. This is the first of many indications that the appearance of the Messiah is accompanied by trouble and distress for others.

Herod's death is mentioned next (2:19), implying some connection with the previous event. But the main clause of the sentence is about the "angel of the Lord" who now tells Joseph that it is safe to return, completing the anticipation of the previous fulfillment quotation (1:15). The message is once again reported in direct speech. Note the words: "the land of Israel" (2:20), which anticipate the journey to Galilee to avoid Archelaus, and to avoid saying that the angel's advice is incorrect, since they will not be safe in Judea. We are told that Joseph is afraid and this fear is confirmed when the angel again warns him. As a result they continue north into Galilee. The appropriateness of this move is then confirmed with a fulfillment quotation: the Messiah is called a Nazarene (2:23).

Matthew 1:17—2:23, usually known as "the Infancy Gospel," has established major elements of the framework of the story. Its primary purpose was to verify the reliability of the narrator who reports to the reader that these events are in full accord with God's intentions. With a minimum of dialogue and with a liberal use of OT quotations, pinpointing the correlation between the OT and these narrated events, the reader is now ready to view Jesus from the "proper" perspective. There can be no doubt about the authority of the narrator, nor can there be any doubt about the Messianic nature of Jesus.

PREPARATION FOR MINISTRY (3:1—4:11)

The second phase in establishing the framework begins with a very vague time reference ("in those days") to introduce John the Baptist's preaching and baptizing (3:1). The reader will assume that it is the same time as that of the previous episode, and it is not until Matt. 3:13 that we realize that Jesus is now an adult. The narrator thereby shows a limited concern for the temporal elements of the story; the primary issue is the divine direction of events. After John the Baptist is introduced and his basic message reported (3:1–2), he is identified as the one who fulfills Isaiah's prophecy (3:3), that is, to announce that the Lord approaches; his primary significance lies in his prophecy. It is only after the fulfillment quotation explains this that John is described in any other way (3:4). His clothing and diet also associate him with the prophets. The people's response to his message is impressive: "Jerusalem and all Judea" (3:5) are baptized.

Typically, the narrator quotes directly. To introduce the quotation, the narrator reports that John criticizes many of the Pharisees and Sadducees who came to him for baptism (3:7). We must assume that they came in response to his message yet he asks them, "Who warned you to flee from the wrath to come?'' This unusual opening is clarified, however, in the next sentence. John adopts a theme that is repeated often in the story—the good fruit. The reader must assume that the deeds of the Pharisees and Sadducees are not commensurate with their intentions; they act as though they are privileged because they are children of Abraham. The reader knows that Jesus himself is not only a descendant of Abraham but is also the Son of God. The contrast is obvious. We can accept John's criticism because he has already been shown to be reliable.

John's understanding of himself is communicated next (3:11–12). Baptism with water precedes baptism by the Messiah; he will baptize with the Holy Spirit. The judgmental aspect of this statement is highlighted by the analogy of the thresher who burns the chaff.

It is only after this portrayal of John that we learn of the connection between John the Baptist and Jesus; Jesus is said to come to John "to be baptized by him" (3:13). John apparently recognizes Jesus and does not want to baptize him. The reader, then, witnesses both John's attitude toward the Pharisees and Sadducees and, in contrast, his attitude toward Jesus. Indeed, John's refusal to baptize is based on a recognition of his own inadequacy.

Jesus' first words in the Gospel of Matthew are short and to the point: "Let it be so now [or 'allow it now'] for thus it is fitting for us to fulfil all righteousness" (3:15). John apparently understands this oblique response because he acquiesces. After the baptism, the Spirit descends and the voice from heaven says: "This is my beloved son, with whom I am well pleased" (3:17).

The reader's first glimpse of Jesus as an adult is this confrontation with a prophet whom we are encouraged to trust. Although it is a short episode, we have enough information about John the Baptist to recognize him as a true Israelite, a man who fears God, and someone who is confident of his point of view. When confronted, however, by the Messiah, whom he seems to recognize, he realizes his limits and, in fact, acts on the basis of his own words. Since Jesus' baptism is greater, it is only obvious that Jesus should baptize him. But notice that we were told that Jesus came to John "to be baptized." And indeed, that is what God wants, as Jesus makes clear and as John eventually realizes. Thus, John the Baptist is pictured in a sympathetic way, similar to Joseph in that he knows the purpose of God will not be denied, even though the required response may not seem appropriate. Later in the Gospel we will hear about "doing the Father's will"; the narrator now depicts this worthy attitude in narrative form.

John's decision to accede to the will of the Father is verified by the voice from heaven. Both Joseph and John are righteous or just men, while the Pharisees and Sadducees are, by contrast, lacking in piety. When John questions Jesus' intention (to be baptized) he asks, "Do you come to me?" (3:13). This is an interesting question because throughout the story "coming to" someone, especially Jesus, is a sign of importance in God's plan, as we will see.

The reader might wonder about God's statement: "with whom I am well pleased." God's pleasure in Jesus must be based on who Jesus is, rather than on what he has done or said. As far as we know, the only thing he has done are those acts just reported in the confrontation with John. We are encouraged, then, by the narrator to accept the authority and reliability of Jesus.

The next episode (4:1–11) follows in temporal sequence and continues this second phase of the introduction. An initial "then" connects it directly to the baptism. The Spirit, who has just alighted on Jesus, now leads him "into the wilderness"—the place where John the Baptist preached (3:1). The temptation "by the devil" is not fortuitous but is planned by God: Jesus is led "to be tempted," just as Jesus came to John "to be baptized."

The privileged position of the narrator is now quite obvious; he or she knows what takes place between Jesus and the devil. We are not told, however, what Jesus' attitude is or what his thoughts are, rather, the narrator only reports the dialogue. Thus the reader must judge the significance of the confrontation on the basis of the information already supplied by the narrator. The primary clue is the narrator's comment that Jesus was led "to be tempted" (4:1). This is reinforced when the devil is called "the tempter" (4:3). Having been thus introduced, the devil's first words are significant: "If you are the son of God" (4:3). The first two temptations begin with this phrase and, of course, reflect the divine declaration at the baptism. Jesus, in response to the appeal to his hunger, quotes from the Book of Deuteronomy (8:3) about living by God's word, not merely by bread. God's word has been prominent in the story, especially in the fulfillment quotations and in the baptismal voice. Here the introductory formula is a simple "it is written" (4:3). Each time Jesus rejects the devil's request, quoting from Deuteronomy, the devil presents another temptation, implying that Jesus has resisted and is indeed following the guidance of the Spirit. After the final temptation, the narrator comments that the devil departed and angels came to minister to Jesus. The cosmic implications of the entire episode are thereby noted. The reader is reminded, then, of the angel of the Lord who directed the action through much of these first chapters.

TRANSITION (4:12–22)

The arrest of John the Baptist causes Jesus to withdraw into Galilee. We get the impression that he may be afraid for his own safety. But in the geographical details about Capernaum, another fulfillment quotation occurs (4:14). The narrator implies that God is in control and that the adult Jesus is fully aligned with God's plan. His withdrawal, then, is not a retreat but a move required by the fact that his preaching career is about to begin. The point of the quotation is that a message of salvation is now available to those who sat in darkness in "Galilee of the Gentiles." Thus, John's arrest is a signal for a beginning, not a retreat. To reinforce this impression, the narrator then summarizes the preaching of Jesus: "From that time Jesus began to preach, saying, 'Repent for the kingdom of heaven is at hand'" (4:17). Since Jesus' message is precisely the same as John's (3:2; 4:17), the continuity between John the Baptist and Jesus is fully affirmed. But the reader already knows that John is the forerunner and that the main phase of God's plan has begun.

As the final element of the framework, the narrator tells the story of the gathering of the first followers (4:18–22). The calling of these four fishermen is told abruptly. It is, of course, puzzling to the reader to be told that these four men simply get up and leave their livelihood. The reader must supply a rationale and the only clue available is the assumption that they are aware of Jesus' message. If so, his invitation would be compelling. They are promised that they will become "fishers of men"—a prediction that is fulfilled at the end of the narrative.

Having read this far, the character of Jesus is now evident to the reader. The one beloved of God, who can withstand the devil's tempting, makes his appeal to common fishermen. It is interesting that his actions have not been described in detail. The meaning of his message is yet to be explained; he is not reported to have had much contact with people; his ability to heal has not been mentioned. Thus the reader has a rather limited description of Jesus. But we are told that the four fishermen left their nets (or boats) and followed him (4:20, 22). In this way, the nature of the story that follows is indicated: Jesus has control over the devil and will make an appeal to humans; he will enlist the help of followers in this attempt to catch "people."

2
The Demands of
the Kingdom

4:23—7:29

The second part of Matthew's story runs from 4:23 through 7:29. After a short introductory report (4:23—5:1), there comes a long speech, the Sermon on the Mount (5:2—7:29). Because the reader now possesses some specific information about Jesus' origins and God's direct involvement in the story, the narrator is now in a position to introduce his teaching.

INTRODUCTORY REPORT (4:23—5:1)

Our interest here is in the function of the Sermon on the Mount as a speech of Jesus within the narrative of this Gospel. This second phase of Matthew's story opens with a broad general statement about Jesus' teaching, his preaching, and his ability to heal "every disease and infirmity among the people" (4:23–25). Although his preaching was mentioned in 4:17, teaching and healing are first noted here. In this way the narrator prepares us for the content of the next five chapters (Matthew 5—9). In addition, the narrator reports that because Jesus' fame has spread throughout Syria, large crowds began to follow him. It is because of this crowd that Jesus goes "up on the mountain" and sits down to teach (5:1). It is not clear whether the narrator intends the reader to picture Jesus' teaching the crowds or just the disciples. Since the disciples are mentioned as coming to him, they are the probable audience. Nevertheless, it is typical of Matthew to portray the crowd as potential followers; this ambiguity about the audience for the Sermon on the Mount is the first indication of this tendency.

THE SERMON ON THE MOUNT (5:2—7:23)

The impact on the reader of a series of direct quotations and especially a speech that is the length of the Sermon on the Mount requires some preliminary comment. The hand of the narrator is, of course, still evident in the choice of the sayings and in their placement. The narrator, however, works indirectly to affect the reader's understanding of, and response to, the individual being quoted. Rather than telling us what the character thinks, or telling us in indirect speech what the narrator understands him to mean, we hear from the person directly. The impact on the reader, therefore, is less direct. In part, the reader's response will be determined by the reliability of the speaker, which the narrator has established.

Since Jesus was portrayed as fully reliable, and since the impact of what he says is very strong, we must ask what insight the reader will gain about Jesus. It is, of course, important to notice when, where, and why he speaks, to whom his words are addressed, and how the addressees react. But the primary question is the overall impact of this combination of material. We could proceed as we have already in the earlier parts of the story, noting the connections between the elements of the speech and their relation to the previous material. But the impact of the speech *as a whole* is just as important. How do we assess it? For this initial speech the reader has only a limited volume of information for comparison; its effect will be primarily constructive. Jesus is presented by the narrator in a less direct way; the narrator lets him speak for himself. Once we have surveyed the content of the speech and its own internal flow, we must then ask how it would affect the reader's perception of Jesus.

Because this is the beginning of Jesus' teaching, and because his message in 4:17 was the same as John's, the contrast and connection between them is important for the reader. John's teaching contained both criticism and warning about the judgment—especially when the Pharisees and Sadducees appear. In contrast, Jesus, preaching the same basic message, is not yet portrayed in confrontation with the Pharisees and Sadducees. Thus, he will strike the reader as less vindictive.

In the opening paragraph, it is clear that he is speaking to disciples and/or potential followers. The form of the opening words, the Beatitudes (5:3–12), would be familiar to a Jewish audience. The first Beatitude promises the kingdom of heaven to the poor in spirit. Having just been informed (4:17) that Jesus' primary message is

"Repent, for the kingdom of heaven is at hand," the continuity of subject matter is obvious and deliberate. Because there is no polemic or criticism of the disciples or the crowd, it follows that the "qualities" that bring God's blessing are those Jesus expects to find in his followers; they are the basis for understanding repentance.

The concluding Beatitude (5:10) stands out because (1) it follows a reference to the kingdom of heaven, (2) it is directed to the audience, and (3) it introduces the theme of persecution. The kingdom of heaven is mentioned and an explicit promise is made: those who follow Jesus, even though persecuted, will receive a great reward in heaven (5:11–12). The circumstances are clear to the reader: Jesus was persecuted as an infant, the prophets were persecuted in the past, and John the Baptist has been arrested. Although the followers' future on earth is dim, the rewards in heaven are assured. Since Jesus is known by the reader to be loved by God, it is easy to accept his word.

The shift from third person plural to second person plural ("you"), introduced in the final Beatitude (5:11–12), continues in the last two sections of Matthew 5 but not as beatitudes. Jesus tells his listeners "you are the salt of the earth" and "the light of the world" (5:13–14). Both sayings emphasize the positive side of the image but do so by referring to the negative; salt that is not salty is as useless as a light that is hidden. The "light" analogy ends with a positive admonition, identifying good works with the brightness of the light and the effect this will have on people, that is, they will "give glory to your Father who is in heaven" (5:16). The specific reference to heaven reminds the reader of the story's ultimate controlling factor.

Jesus' next statement comes as a surprise. We are told not to think that he has come "to abolish the law and the prophets but to fulfill them" (5:17). We have to assume that someone has made such an accusation, but why they might do so has not been narrated. In fact, the narrator has, to this point in the story, reported (1) repeated references that show how events in Jesus' life have fulfilled the sayings of the prophets, (2) how his place of birth was predicted by them, and (3) that he vanquished the devil, using a judicious series of quotations from the law. Thus, the reader can appreciate the truth of the denial and look forward to its verification. The next sentence (5:18) affirms and reinforces his respect for the Scripture. Its force is heightened by the formal introduction ("For truly, I say to you"); the reader is thereby reminded of the basis of his authority and his reliability. Notice the future dimension of the promise: "Until all is accomplished." The reader is being reminded of the way the fulfillment quotations align present events with statements from the past. The only clues the reader has for anticipating exactly what this accomplishment will be are (1) the name given to Jesus in Matt. 1:21 ("for he will save his people") and (2) the predominant use of the kingdom of heaven, both as an element of the future and as an aspect of the will of God.

Jesus next warns his audience of the danger of neglecting these commands (5:19–20). The focus is still on the kingdom of heaven; one's status within it will depend on one's fulfillment of the commands. In fact, he says, you cannot enter the kingdom of heaven "unless your righteousness exceeds that of the scribes and Pharisees" (5:20). At this point in the narrative the reader's evaluation of the Pharisees and Sadducees is dependent upon John the Baptist's earlier criticism (3:7–12). We know they are enemies or opponents of some sort. This statement is a backhanded compliment which implies that they are somewhat righteous; they have not reached the full limits of righteousness. Since we already know that Joseph was "just" and that John acceded to Jesus' request to "fulfill all righteousness," the meaning of the word "righteousness" is being developed.

It should also be noted that the focus of the opening portions of the speech (Beatitudes and two analogies of salt and light) is upon the kingdom of heaven, while this paragraph focuses on Jesus himself. The arrangement is significant: it establishes a correlation between the two.

ANTITHESES (5:21–48)

The next section of the Sermon on the Mount (5:21–48) contains the well-known antitheses. Without any pause, Jesus presents six examples of what it means to fulfill the law and the prophets. Five of these sayings begin with a reference to information that the hearers already possess. All six sayings have the same structure: a reference to the Jewish tradition about God's will followed by the antithesis "but I say to you." The last three of these statements are reported in direct speech; the result is a strengthening of the reader's perception of Jesus' authority.

The antithesis is a strong rhetorical device which will have a pronounced effect upon the reader, coming, as it does, after Jesus has affirmed his obedience to the law. It is unclear whether Jesus is quoting from the sayings of the Pharisees or not. Nevertheless, the effect is striking: God's word is not to be interpreted in a legalistic way but as a radical guide to conduct. The example of the man at the altar (5:23–24) focuses on the one who performs a religious act. One can imagine that the reader will see the connection between Jesus and the prophets who confronted all hypocrites. Their attack on sacrifice and false security was already echoed in the portrait of John the Baptist; thus the continuity between Jesus and John is developed further. The short reference to an accuser (5:25–26) in a court case functions in a similar way. The first antithesis concludes with a warning, introduced with a formula ("truly, I say to you," v.26), about the dire consequences of ignoring this advice.

The second antithesis (5:27–30) also radicalizes the law: lustful looks are equated with adultery in the heart. The extreme consequences, being thrown into hell, require drastic action such as cutting off one's hand.

The other four antitheses concern divorce (5:31–32), taking of oaths (5:33–37), retribution (5:38–42), and love of enemies (5:43–48). It is the last of these contrast-sayings that will perhaps have the most impact on the reader. In it the basic theme of the discourse is repeated, the kingdom of heaven. Although the word "kingdom" is not used, the narrator reports that Jesus advises his followers that love of one's enemy will bring them to sonship with "your Father who is in heaven" (v.45). Because we are all God's creatures, obedience to the Father is required. Although tax collectors and Gentiles perform deeds that are to their own advantage, the heavenly Father requires more. To be a child of God one must be perfect. This conclusion stands out for the reader because of a change in pace. It is only here that rhetorical questions appear, a device well-known for attracting attention. This change in the rhythm, with the audacious statement about perfection at its conclusion, will certainly jar the reader. The radical demands Jesus presents in this section certainly help to explain the warning in 5:20: one's righteousness must exceed that of the scribes and Pharisees. We know what John the Baptist thinks of the Pharisees and Sadducees. Now we find that Jesus is just as harsh.

TRUE PIETY (6:1–34)

Having been informed about the need for perfection required by the Father, the next sentence (6:1) follows naturally. "Practicing piety" is an apt description of how some might try to achieve a righteousness which exceeds that of the scribes and Pharisees. Just as the antitheses supply six examples of what Jesus means by fulfillment of the law and prophets, following the summary of 5:17–20, the narrator now presents three examples of true piety.

The first concerns giving alms (6:2–4). The saying contrasts the reader with the hypocrites, who are readily equated with the scribes and Pharisees. The refrain focuses on the importance of an action rather than its public visibility. Since it is the Father who rewards us, it is his evaluation that is significant.

The second example (6:5–15) follows the same pattern, this time about prayer; it is illustrated with an example (the Lord's Prayer) which includes the words about the "Gentiles' empty phrases" as a further negative example.

The third example (6:16–18) is about fasting. The hypocrites are, again, the negative model. Repetition like this has its effect on the reader. Each prohibition ends with an emphasis on the Father's capacity to see "in secret." Thus, when the next verse (6:19) begins with a prohibition, the flow of material is not interrupted; the specific problem is material goods but the saying contrasts impermanence with a correct and consistent piety. In this context, then, treasures in heaven are clearly the attitudes recommended in the six antitheses and the three "pieties." The mention of "heart" in 6:21 and the symbolic use of eye and body imagery in 6:22–23 combine to encourage the reader to expect a parabolic use of language.

Matt. 6:24 serves as a summary: no one can serve two masters, God and mammon. The implication is that the hypocrites try to serve both and, as a result, fall far short of God's demands. To pull these themes together, then, the narrator reports Jesus' words about anxiety (6:25–34), introducing them with a "therefore." Since it is assumed that the hearers are indeed anxious about food and clothing, calling them "men of little faith" (v.30) underlines the basic theme of doubleness, trying to serve God and mammon. Another reference to the Father in heaven reminds us that Jesus speaks from God's point of view; he is the fulfiller of the law and prophets. Jesus closes by stating the correct priorities: "Seek first his kingdom and his righteousness" (6:33).

CONCLUSION (7:1–27)

The final section of the Sermon on the Mount opens with a series of direct demands accompanied by illustrations that warn of the negative results: do not judge; watch for the beam in your own eye (notice that "hypocrite" is now applied to the listener); do not give what is holy to dogs, lest it be trampled. To ask is to receive: God will give. The overall theme of the Sermon on the Mount is specified in the Golden Rule (7:12) which Jesus says *is* the law and the prophets, a reminder of what was important at the beginning of the sermon (5:17–20).

Finally, Jesus explains how difficult it is to travel this path; it is like finding a narrow gate (7:13). One could be misled by false prophets who are indeed hypocrites, or double-minded (7:15–20). They appear to be followers, but their lack of integrity is known by the Father. Then Jesus says he will be called Lord and will act as a judge (7:22). Thus the narrator has influenced the reader to recognize Jesus' status in addition to his God-given authority.

The Sermon on the Mount ends with the famous parable of the two builders (7:24–27). The house built on sand falls; it represents the hypocrite. The person whose deeds are consistent with Jesus' own words, which are the Father's words, and which therefore fulfill the law and prophets, will survive the time of distress and punishment.

The narrator's summary (7:28–29) states that the crowds were astonished, for he taught with authority, "not as their scribes." By using the word "their," the narrator implies that the crowd has recognized the point of Jesus' attack.

What will be the reader's image of Jesus after reading the Sermon on the Mount? There is certainly no problem of consistency. The message of Jesus here does not differ from our earlier perception of him. He is direct and forthright and he is obviously an astute observer of nature and of people. Most important, perhaps, is the impression that Jesus views the world from above—from a cosmic perspective, so to speak. His words help to reinforce his divine status; what had earlier been stated has now been illustrated in the narrative.

3

The Power of the Kingdom

8:1—11:1

After introducing the reader to Jesus' message by means of the sayings in Matthew 5—7, the narration resumes with a comment about the crowds who continue to follow him (8:1), just as they had before he began to speak (4:25). Here, as there, the immediate context is a healing. The report in 8:2–4 is different in that the diseased person comes to Jesus himself, rather than being brought by others (4:24–25). The reader is encouraged to view the leper as part of the crowd which, after the Sermon on the Mount, is convinced that Jesus can heal. The conditional clause, "if you will" (v. 2), in the request is echoed in Jesus' response, "I will" (v. 3); the cleansing is immediate. In this report, the narrator reminds us that Jesus' power and authority enable him both to teach and also to heal. Jesus' motives are not explained; we are left to wonder whether he is reacting to the disease or perhaps to the way he is addressed. We *are* given some indication of Jesus' attitude in his concluding comment: the healed leper is told to remain silent about the source of his health and to offer the sacrifice "that Moses commanded" (8:4). After the narrator's emphasis on Jesus' obedience to the law and its fulfillment in the Sermon on the Mount, he demonstrates that Jesus acts in accord with his preaching—Jesus is not a hypocrite. Obviously the miracle could be a way of attracting attention but he does not want it interpreted as such.

As Jesus enters Capernaum (8:5), a centurion approaches and reports that his servant is ill. Once again Jesus' reply emphasizes that he chooses to heal. The centurion also calls him Lord. Both the leper (8:2–4) and the centurion are "outsiders" in this society, yet Jesus willingly responds to their needs. This point is emphasized by the narrator who details the remarkable statement of the centurion which, in effect, underlines the significance of the narrator's comment at the end of the Sermon on the Mount (7:28–29) about the authority of Jesus. This is the first time since John the Baptist (3:1–12) that we are informed of an individual's response to Jesus. Its importance is stressed when Jesus praises the centurion for exhibiting a faith that exceeds the faith of the Jews he has encountered. The contrast between Gentile and Jew is further highlighted by the emphatic comment (8:11–12) about the future kingdom. "Abraham, Isaac, and Jacob" will remind the reader of the genealogy. The "sons of the kingdom," ejected and condemned (8:12), are the unresponsive Jews. The centurion's comment, then, focuses our attention on Jesus' authority while the healing is almost an anticlimax. It is the centurion's faith that Jesus himself emphasizes in the conclusion (8:13). But the narrator goes one step farther: Jesus speaks first to his followers and then to the centurion. As a result the reader will maintain a distinction between the centurion and Jesus' followers. Second, the saying serves as an interpretation—like an aside in a play—for the reader's benefit.

After another notice of a change in location (8:14), the narrator reports that Jesus healed Peter's mother-in-law, offering little information about her response. Then, that evening, in apparently the same location, "many who were possessed of demons" are healed (8:16). We are reminded again of the healing reported in the summary at 4:24, just before the Sermon on the Mount. The same phrase, "all who are sick," is used in both places (4:24; 8:16).

This demonstration of power is followed by a fulfillment quotation (8:17), the first since the summary about Jesus' activity in Galilee (4:14–16). The narrator is reminding the reader of the basic framework of the story. Jesus does not act "on his own" but in accord with God's plan and intention. The correlation between God's plan and Jesus' action is just as close as that between God's will and Jesus' teaching.

IN GENTILE TERRITORY (8:18–34)

At Matt. 8:18 the narrator informs us that Jesus decides to go across the lake when he sees the crowds gathered about him. Whether he perceives them as threatening, or annoying, or as a sign of his success, we are left to imagine. The following verse, however, confirms that the narrator is not interested in why Jesus moves on, but rather in the fact that he does not settle down in any one location (v. 19). The scribe who approaches him claims to be a potential follower. However, Jesus reacts to his comment with a saying that warns him of the consequences: such a decision is likely to lead to constant wandering and its concomitant—"homelessness." Another disciple, apparently inspired by the scribe's dedication, but also anticipating the demands that Jesus presents, asks to be allowed to attend his father's funeral (v. 21). Jesus' response is indeed harsh. The primary requirement is boldly stated: "Follow me." All this precedes the actual crossing to the other side; the disciples literally "followed" Jesus (8:23). The great storm (8:24–27) that threatens their lives does not disturb Jesus; when awakened, he rebukes both the storm and his followers. In this way we know that they have not learned the lesson of the two sayings nor have they heeded the earlier advice about the futility of anxiety (6:25–34). Their request, "Save, Lord; we are perishing" (v. 25), is a prayer. Jesus, answering in the midst of the storm, comments on their "little faith" before he calms the storm. This is the first time that we encounter the power of Jesus over natural phenomena; earlier healings were put in the context of his control over demons. Jesus' compassion is balanced by his demands. The question at the end of the incident, "What sort of man is this?" (8:27), is, of course, ironic for the reader. We know his origins and credentials; the disciples do not yet comprehend. Nevertheless, because they are the people who follow, we are left to wonder why. They have witnessed him healing and they have heard his extraordinary demands, but they apparently do not anticipate this kind of control over the world.

Jesus, the narrator tells us (8:28), having crossed the lake, now enters non-Jewish territory. He is met by two demoniacs (8:28–34) who terrorize the cemetery they inhabit. Typically, they recognize Jesus as Son of God, as the devil himself did (4:3), and are immediately on the defensive. Because the narrator informs us that a herd of swine is nearby, the reader will assume that their question implies that they recognize their precarious situation. They ask to be transferred into the swine, an indication of how desperate they really are. Jesus merely says, "Go." The immediate drowning of the swine demonstrates how self-destructive these demons really are. The report of the herdsmen and the subsequent request of the townspeople informs the reader that some Gentiles recognized Jesus' power and the extent of his authority. Jesus honors their request and returns to "his own city."

Thus, Jesus enters foreign territory because of the crowds, but his show of power there leads another crowd to ask him to leave. Because the narrator does not tell us what Jesus' own thoughts are, merely that he accedes to their request, the reader is encouraged to confirm Jesus' authority. "Healing" includes (1) healing proper, (2) control over the forces of nature, and (3) control over demons. In Matthew 8 there is little emphasis on teaching.

When Jesus returns to Capernaum, the infirm continue to be brought to him; this time the narrator focuses on a paralytic. And for the second time, the narrator specifically mentions the faith of the bearers; earlier (8:5–13) it was the faith of the centurion. Here, we are merely informed that Jesus "saw their faith" (9:2); we are left to wonder how he knew.

IN GALILEE (9:1–34)

Jesus' words (9:2) are unexpected: "Take heart, my son; your sins are forgiven." The only times the word "sins" was mentioned earlier in the story was in the definition of the name of Jesus: "For he will save his people from their sins" (1:21), and when John the Baptist castigated the Pharisees and Sadducees (3:6). The connection between sins and paralysis is not questioned or commented on. Rather, the narrator tells us that "some of the scribes said to themselves, 'This man is blaspheming'" (9:3). Although we do not know at this point precisely what they mean, we are told that Jesus knew their thoughts. This is one of the few times that the narrator has given the reader any direct indication of Jesus' own ability to "read minds." It comes as no shock, however. It adds further weight to the reader's impression of the authority of both Jesus and the narrator.

Jesus' reaction to this unvoiced accusation is to ask two rhetorical questions (9:4–5) to emphasize his own authority. In a situation where Jesus' ability and authority have been recognized and acknowledged by a variety of individuals, the scribes' own resistance is highlighted. First, Jesus says that their resistance is "evil" and second, that its source is in their hearts, a reference to the Sermon on the Mount (6:21). The quality of "evil" is then qualified in Jesus' second question about whether it is easier to forgive or to heal. Thus Jesus, who came to save his people from their sins, does indeed save them when he heals. This correlation is portrayed when he commands the paralytic to rise and go home. Jesus refers to himself as the Son of man for the second time, previously in 8:20. The Son of man, described here as homeless, is also one with God-given authority. The healing itself is reported in a very matter-of-fact way. But the significance for the narrator is illustrated in the conclusion. The crowds, we are told, recognize the importance of what Jesus has done, both the healing and the rebuke of the scribes, and they react with awe, as though in the presence of God or one who receives power from God.

The narrator's art is visible, then, in the use of direct quotation and in the infrequent use of "omniscience." The reader is encouraged to recognize Jesus as a legitimate healer by means of the varied reactions of his contemporaries. The religious establishment is portrayed as consistently obstructive, attempting to thwart or pester him.

While Jesus is still in Capernaum, the narrator reports that Jesus sees Matthew, a tax collector, and invites him to follow (9:9). And he does! We have no clue about why he would do such a rash thing—no motives or explanation. The reader must supply a rationale from the context. In 5:46, the tax collectors were presented as examples of those people, like the Gentiles, who act in their own self-interest. Since "tax collector" is virtually a synonym for sinner, the narrator is contrasting the response of a sinner to the obtuseness of the scribes; the tax collector responds positively to the authority of Jesus, mentioned by the narrator in the previous verse (9:8). Not only does *this* tax collector follow; we are told that "many tax collectors and sinners" came to eat with Jesus (9:10). The narrator has thereby set the stage for the Pharisees' question to the disciples about why Jesus does "this," implying that it is not acceptable behavior. When Jesus either overhears or is told about it (the point is not clear in the text), he responds as follows: first, with a proverb about the sick needing a physician (v. 12); second, with a command about mercy (v. 13, based on a quotation from a prophet); and third, that he came to call sinners, not the righteous (v. 13).

The dinner conversation continues (9:14) when John the Baptist's disciples ask about the discrepancy between their practice of fasting, also important to the Pharisees, and Jesus' disciples who do not fast, an appropriate question at a meal. Jesus' reply is indirect, that is, he uses three analogies: one about the inappropriateness of fasting during a wedding (v. 15); another about a patch of new cloth put on an old garment (v. 16); and third, one about new wine put into old wineskins (v. 17). None of these comparisons is explained and the reader must supply the connection. A multiple appeal to common practices, when juxtaposed like this, is a direct invitation to the reader to seek the common element. In each instance it is a matter of adapting to existing conditions, as the first analogy states. Jesus' action, and what he recommends for his followers, is activity that is sensible because of who he is. Jesus had already said (5:16–18) that fasting is not wrong, but should be done righteously and in secret. Since the announcement of the kingdom of heaven is his primary message (4:13), it is apparent that the approach of the kingdom demands appropriate action.

The vague introduction to the next episode (9:18) is another indication of the narrator's lack of interest in complete "stage directions." The reader will assume that Jesus is still at his home when the "ruler" asks him to come raise his daughter from death. The narrator mentions that Jesus "followed him, with his disciples" (v. 15). On the way a woman who had suffered from a hemorrhage for twelve years touches his garment (v. 20). The narrator not only makes certain that the reader knows how serious her problem was, but also explains her motive, in direct speech, by quoting her thoughts: she expects to be healed. Jesus, responding to her touch, knows what she wants. Thus, without saying it directly, the narrator has shown us how perceptive Jesus is. When he says that it is her faith that has made her well, we can be certain of the truth of this judgment. This is the third time (8:10; 9:2, 22) that faith has been mentioned in connection with a healing, but it is the first time that the faith of the person healed is noted. The reader cannot miss this close connection. The faith that brings healing is apparently a confidence that Jesus can do what only a man with divine authority can do. The cure, effected immediately, is reported in a casual way while Jesus continues on his way.

Upon arriving at the ruler's house, the crowd's tumultuous mourning is mentioned (9:23). Yet they laugh when Jesus claims that the daughter is merely asleep. But the reader knows what Jesus can do. Nevertheless, one must wonder whether Jesus has *this* kind of authority, to revive the dead. After the crowd is dismissed, Jesus raises her by merely taking her hand. The narrator finishes by saying that this raising was reported throughout all that district of Galilee around Capernaum (v. 25).

Notice that one incident (9:20–22) is enclosed within another (9:18–19; and 9:23–26), a technique that encourages the reader to seek the connection between them. Although the faith of the ruler is not mentioned, he shows the same confidence in Jesus' authority that the woman with the hemorrhage shows. Thus the narrator implies that even hopeless situations, such as these, are not beyond Jesus' power, provided there is confidence in Jesus, "who will save his people." Jesus demonstrates that he has a mercy the Pharisees do not possess.

After another vague transitional note, the narrator reports the healing of two blind men (9:27–31). They follow Jesus, shouting, "Have mercy on us, Son of David." Mercy, which Jesus has already extolled (9:13), is now the basis of their request. Calling Jesus "Son of David" recalls, of course, the genealogy and the story of Jesus' origins, that part of the narrative which established the reader's confidence in Jesus' authority. There is an interesting change in the pattern at this point: Jesus goes into a house (his own?) to question the blind men, asking if they believe (have faith) that he can "do this." They answer, "Yes, Lord." Thus the matter of faith, which has increased in frequency, is now directly stated by the narrator. And when Jesus responds that God will act according to "their faith," the narrator has put the issue of faith directly on the lips of Jesus. The unusual phrase, "be it done unto you" (v. 29), is an oblique way of reminding the reader that Jesus does these things as a representative of the Father and not on his own.

After the healing, Jesus "charges" them not to make it known, but the narrator reports that they spread his fame anyway (9:30–31). This will indeed puzzle the reader; one would expect that a person who understands the divine source of Jesus' authority would heed such a request. That they do not is an indication to the reader that those who profess faith, and apparently have some understanding of Jesus, do not always act in accord with his wishes. As the gospel narrative proceeds, we will see further indications of this apparent inconsistency. It has already been hinted at in the denunciation of the Pharisees and in the action of the disciples in the boat (8:18–23).

Another vague plot notice leads to still another confrontation between Jesus and someone in need, this time a man possessed by a demon (9:32–34). The narrator reports the exorcism in as concise a way as possible in order to get to the main point: the contrast between the reaction of the crowds and the Pharisees. Both the crowd and the Pharisees are quoted, speaking for themselves. However, because the crowd is first described as marveling, the narrator has constructed a context which helps the reader assess their open-ended comment. The Pharisees are simply quoted; their comment is a judgment: "He casts out demons by the Prince of demons" (9:34). Thus the narrator confirms what was expected: the Pharisees now explicitly oppose

Jesus. They speak not only against Jesus himself but against his authority, an authority that many others have recognized. They become examples of nonfaith since the reader has often seen how Jesus' words and actions complement each other. The Pharisees' accusation is obviously perverse; Jesus does not abolish the law and the prophets but fulfills them. Thus the reader is prepared for the conflict that will follow.

TRANSITION (9:35—10:4)

Matt. 9:35 is virtually identical to the earlier statement about how Jesus preaches, teaches, and heals (4:23), reminding the reader of the three main facets of Jesus' activity. It is the crowd that has responded to him and the narrator now tells us, as he seldom does, Jesus' thought and motivation: he has compassion on the crowd because they are harassed and helpless like sheep without a shepherd (9:36). This comment will have a powerful effect on the reader because so far the narrator has provided little insight into the mind of Jesus. In effect, we are supplied with an interpretive context for the saying which follows. The "harvest" must be the culmination of the teaching, preaching, and healing of Jesus; the disciples are requested to pray for its successful completion, that these helpless and harassed people might be cared for by the Father.

Having then associated the image of harvest and laborers with the helpless people and the disciples, the narrator reports that Jesus called twelve of the followers to be disciples, giving them authority to both exorcise and heal (10:1). This is the first time the narrator has mentioned the Twelve, a group selected from the wider company of followers. To reinforce their distinctiveness, their names are listed; notice that they are called "apostles" in 10:2, the only time this title appears in Matthew's story, and this encourages the reader to think of these chosen followers as messengers. The combination of terms is not unusual; the correlation between being and acting is typical of the story. The first four disciples were introduced before (chap.4), and Matthew was mentioned before (chap. 9). The other names are new. Some are identified by their family ties, one by his occupation, and one by his background (Simon the Zealot). By calling Judas Iscariot the one "who betrayed him," the narrator anticipates Jesus' death but in a way that simply states what will happen, not merely hints. That is, by using the past tense, the narrator not only reports what will happen but indicates that his point of view is the same as that expressed in the formula quotations.

THE MISSION DISCOURSE (10:5-42)

The twelve "apostles" are "sent out" with instructions. The discourse begins at 10:5 even though the narrator began preparing us for it in 9:36; the helpless people are about to be visited by the Twelve, the messengers of Jesus. Notice that the narrator does not mention that they are to teach. Rather, they have authority to exorcise and heal, and they are asked to "preach" the message of the nearness of the kingdom of heaven, with almost the same words that John and Jesus used: "Repent, for the kingdom of heaven is at hand" (3:2; 4:17).

Specific instructions for the mission (10:5-15) begin in a conventional way: the Twelve are told to concentrate their efforts on the "lost sheep of the house of Israel" (10:6) and *not* to go among the Gentiles or Samaritans. This command is not unexpected. We were told, from the beginning, of Jesus' Jewish background and the focus of his action. Although a few Gentiles have been praised or have played a positive role, the emphasis of both the Sermon on the Mount and Jesus' activity (chaps. 8—9) has been directed to his own people. Also, among the Twelve, those we know about are Jews. They must work among their own people.

Their specific task is described with two verbs: "preach" and "heal." The message is one we have heard before, about the approach of the kingdom but now without the exhortation, "Repent!" The reader is already acquainted with it from the Sermon on the Mount. The authority to heal (cf. 10:1) is repeated in 10:8, now as a specific command of Jesus. The Twelve should follow his example as explained in the Sermon on the Mount and narrated in Matthew 8—9.

The following statement about payment (10:8) is equally important: the reward is the doing of it, because of the authority they have just received. This point is then elaborated in 10:9-10 which notes that the fate of the mission depends on the response of the people. The Twelve must travel without money or material resources. The narrator implies that the reader should recognize his own role in this situation when he stresses that recipients should be "worthy." We were told in 3:8, when John the Baptist castigated the Pharisees and Sadducees, that he demanded fruit "worthy of repentance." Thus the idea of repentance was already associated with the word "worthy" and it is implied here. Thus, the advice given to the Twelve also informs the reader; the missionaries who come to them should be welcomed. "Being worthy" applies both to the disciples and to the reader. If the Twelve are not received openly and hospitably, they must leave, showing their disdain by shaking the dust from their feet. These first instructions end with a warning (10:15) that anticipates the day of judgment when such action is punished. The threat of judgment, a major item in the Sermon on the Mount, is repeated here with the introductory emphasis, "Truly, I say to you."

Now that a negative side of the mission has been mentioned, the remainder of this speech (10:16–42) develops that point. The instructions were short and to the point: where to go, what to say and do, and how to support oneself. From 10:16 on, Jesus warns the Twelve that they will not be welcomed by everyone. Even though they serve the Son of God who has authority and knowledge, they will not be accepted. In fact, they will not only be mistreated, they will also cause considerable turmoil wherever they go.

This dramatic shift in emphasis from instruction to warning is introduced by a proverbial statement: "Behold, I send you out as sheep in the midst of wolves" (10:16). This generalization is followed by a series of specific predictions that make it clear that persecution will come from both Jews and Gentiles. Jesus advises: don't be anxious about what to say, the Father will assist you with his Spirit even though intrafamily rivalries will result. Thus, the major part of the mission discourse describes not what the apostles should do, or their mission technique, but rather informs the reader that Jesus is aware of the troubles ahead. The "missionaries" must be warned about it. Twice (10:20, 22) there are statements to encourage the apostles: God is with you to assist you in your speaking, and, those who endure will be rewarded.

Another proverbial saying occurs in 10:24: master and disciple are similar. If the master is maligned, so also the servant. This, then, is followed by the Beelzebul accusation (v. 25) which will be repeated later in detail. It serves as a way of piquing the reader's interest and anticipating the problems to come, both for Jesus and for the apostles.

The ominous tone continues with a statement about fear, also with a proverbial flavor (10:26). Now the issue is not merely persecution or slander, but death. Jesus tells the Twelve to fear the one with full control over life, not those with partial control. As we have come to expect, the emphasis has shifted to the Father; he is concerned about such minor things as sparrows (10:29) and hair (10:30), even though he is the judge of the world. Thus, after the warning, the crucial point is made: acknowledgment and denial determine one's fate.

The mission is potentially disruptive (10:34–38). The "sword" is explained in terms of intrafamily conflict, elicited by the heavy demands Jesus places on his followers. "Worthy" (10:37) appears again, as at the beginning of the speech (10:11), but now extended ("worthy of me") and defined: one must leave family and be willing to take up his cross. The warning ends with the proverbial paradox about losing one's life to find it "for my sake" (10:39).

The conclusion (10:40–42) of the mission discourse begins with another proverbial saying. It sums up the basic theme of the speech but with the emphasis again on the positive side. Receiving Jesus means receiving the one who sent him. This point is expanded with two examples: (1) receiving a prophet as a prophet, that is, as a person guided by the Father, will bring a prophet's reward; (2) receiving a righteous man as righteous, that is, as a person who does what the Father requires, will also bring an appropriate reward. But, since the next sentence (10:42) implies that these are "little ones" who may be in need, as indeed the messengers truly are in need, helping the messengers is equivalent to helping Jesus himself. Receiving them means to welcome and assist them. Notice, however, the change in the addressee: the last verse (v. 42) is addressed to the "crowd" with the implication that Jesus gestures to the "apostles" as the "little ones." This is another indication of the way the narrator places the reader in the crowd. And we will encounter the same theme, that is, helping others as equivalent to helping Jesus at the end of his final speech (25:31–46).

In conclusion, we must ask what overall effect this speech will have on the reader. In addition to slowing down the pace of the narrative, the narrator has reminded us of many of the themes and issues that were introduced in the Sermon on the Mount (chaps. 5—7) and the narration in Matthew 8—9. The most important feature, however, is the shift in emphasis toward the problems and difficulties that lie ahead. Since Jesus' reliability is firmly established, his warnings and predictions carry the weight of certainty. Thereby the reader is forcefully reminded of the close connection between Jesus and the authority of the Father.

4

The Response to the Coming of the Kingdom

11:1—18:35

Matthew 11 marks the beginning of a new phase of the narrative. In addition to forcing a break in the continuity of the story, there are new demands placed upon the reader to fill in narrative gaps. This readjustment begins immediately in 11:1 when the narrator tells us that after Jesus finished instructing the Twelve, he left on a teaching and preaching mission of his own. Notice that there is no mention of any healing. Moreover, the narrator does not say a word about the departure of the disciples nor are we told whether they did what Jesus requested. Also, the Twelve are called disciples not apostles. Therefore, we must assume from 10:5 that they do indeed fulfill the command to preach. "Their" cities, the places Jesus preaches (11:1), grammatically refers to the cities of the disciples but could refer to the cities of the Pharisees (cf. "their synagogues," 9:35).

These indeterminacies will require the reader to apply the information already narrated to establish continuity. In addition, 11:1 is similar to the two previous summary statements (4:23; 9:36) and adds to the impression that a new phase of the story is beginning

JOHN THE BAPTIST IS UNCERTAIN (11:2–19)

When the next verse (11:2) informs us that John the Baptist, who is in prison, sends his disciples to Jesus to ask if Jesus is indeed the one who is to come, the reader again must readjust. This is the first we have heard of John's imprisonment; it continues one of the themes of the previous speech, that persecution is indeed imminent. But John's question is unexpected. We were told earlier that John was convinced by Jesus that he should baptize him (3:13–15) and, in addition, John was told by the voice from heaven that Jesus is the beloved Son of God. Now, perhaps because of his imprisonment and because he has heard of "the deeds of the Christ," John is unsure. Thus the reader's interest is raised by this unanticipated doubt. The narrator, however, colors our view of Jesus' authority by referring to him as the "Christ." This title has not been used by anyone in the narrative so far, only by the narrator in the opening of the story (chaps. 1 and 2). Thus we are inclined to assume that John the Baptist is wrong and that he does not hold up under persecution, as Jesus had advised the disciples (10:39). Jesus answers John's query immediately (11:4–6), using language reminiscent of his commission to the apostles (10:5–8) and which also echoes the words of Isaiah 29 and 35. Although Matt. 11:1 did not mention healing, the miraculous deeds of Jesus (called "Christ" by the narrator) are brought to the reader's attention. By implication, then, John is admonished for failing to maintain his initial confidence and he is also subtly reminded that Jesus fulfills the promises of the prophet. Although this allusion is not a formal fulfillment quotation (a narrator's technique), it functions in a similar way. It has the authority of Jesus and confirms what the narrator has been saying on his own. The final sentence of Jesus' answer (11:6) is a beatitude which implies that John should be criticized for his lack of confidence. John was looking for the one who would come after him; he now doubts that Jesus is that "one." The reader, in turn, is inclined to reassess his positive opinion of John the Baptist.

Once the implied criticism of John the Baptist is stated, Jesus addresses the crowds (11:7–24). He first asks a series of questions which clearly imply a positive evaluation of John, not the negative one of the previous saying. No one would go out into the wilderness to find a reed shaken in the wind! No one, by analogy, goes out into the wilderness to see a well-dressed person; instead, they would go to a palace. The crowds, who went to see John, went to see a prophet and "more than a prophet" (11:9). Jesus then quotes Mal. 3:1, implying that John the Baptist is the preparatory messenger. Thus Jesus is reported to use a method of argumentation (the quotation of prophecy) that the narrator himself repeatedly employs to verify the accuracy of his analogies.

Such a paradoxical evaluation of John the Baptist encourages the reader to look for the underlying rationale. The difficulty continues, however, in the next saying. John is praised as the greatest of humans and yet he is less than even the least in the kingdom of heaven (11:11). Aside from the unexplained assumption that there are degrees or levels within the kingdom, the primary distinction is between humans here and the inhabitants of the kingdom. Since both Jesus and John preach about the coming of the kingdom, and because Jesus is associated with the coming of the kingdom, the reader is encouraged to view John as the end of the pre-kingdom era. This tendency is reinforced in the next statement about violence: the days of John the Baptist are over and, subsequently, violence has increased (11:12); and this comes in the context of Jesus' warning in Matthew 10 about violence and persecution. "All the prophets and the law prophesied *until* John," he says (11:13). But Jesus then says that although it is difficult to comprehend or accept John the Baptist "is Elijah who is to come. He who has ears to hear, let him hear" (11:14–15). The reader is warned both by the conditional sentence ("if you are willing") and by the final admonition ("he who has ears . . .") to interpret the saying carefully. John the Baptist *is* the forerunner and, as a result, he is the final expression of prophecy. John's role at the opening of the narrative was to acknowledge Jesus as the Messiah and to witness the heavenly announcement that Jesus is God's Son. Here in chap. 11 his function as forerunner is again affirmed, even though his doubts are condemned. John has succumbed to the pressure of persecution despite Jesus' advice and warning.

Jesus continues to speak to the crowd in 11:16 but he changes the subject to "this generation," presumably the source of the violence mentioned in 11:2. "This generation" is compared to children who are never able to control their playmates; they want to "call the tune" and determine the game that is to be played; when they can't, they complain. This generation has called John the Baptist, the ascetic, a demoniac; Jesus, the nonascetic, they call a glutton, because he associates with outcasts. This section ends when Jesus asserts, "Wisdom is justified by her deeds" (11:19), that is, wisdom is manifest not primarily in sayings but in actions. The word "deeds" reminds us of the narrator's statement in 11:2 that John the Baptist asked about Jesus' identity because of the "deeds" of the Christ— most likely a reference to the teaching and miracles narrated in chaps. 8 and 9.

Matthew 11 is, therefore, pivotal in guiding the reader. It demonstrates how John the Baptist, who was so important in the early part of the story and who was described as a prophet, is now both criticized and praised. John lacks full commitment; those who have not yet entered the kingdom of heaven will also be imperfect.

FURTHER REACTIONS TO JESUS (11:20–24)

John's wavering appears less serious, however, when in the next section of the narrative (11:20–24) Jesus "upbraids" or curses the inhabitants of some of the unrepentant villages of Galilee. Matt. 11:20 is an explanatory summary from the narrator. "Repent" is, of course, closely associated with the coming of the kingdom (cf. 4:17) and is the narrator's deliberate way of helping the reader interpret the following criticism. In 11:21–24 Jesus is angry, in contrast to his attitude toward John the Baptist. And, furthermore, these villages of Galilee are compared unfavorably with the gentile cities of Tyre, Sidon, and Sodom. The repeated reference to the day of judgment reinforces for the reader the importance of the response. But the comparative form ("more tolerable") implies that one's misdeeds are evaluated in relation to the deeds of others.

THE SON'S AUTHORITY AND TASK (11:25–30)

Matt. 11:25 contains another of the narrator's vague temporal references: "at that time." Since this entire sequence of sayings (11:3–24) has been addressed to the crowd (11:7), we must assume that the crowds can hear when Jesus now speaks to the Father. Calling the Father "Lord of heaven and earth" reminds the reader of Jesus' origins and character in addition to his message about the coming of the kingdom of heaven. These verses also continue the narrator's emphasis on the presence of the Father. When Jesus affirms that God both hides and reveals "these things" to a certain group (11:25), he reaffirms God's control over events, as in the fulfillment quotations and the birth story. The Son is known only by those who have been granted this knowledge by God. And it follows naturally that Jesus specifically issues an invitation to the crowd to come to him and to accept his yoke and his rest (11:29). Note also that the taking of the yoke is parallel to "learn from me" *(Mathete)*; the word for disciple is *Mathētēs*, that is, a learner who comes to Jesus. This theme will be expanded later.

THE OPPOSITION INCREASES (12:1-14)

Although 11:25-30 appears to be a conclusion, this section of the narrative is not yet over; the introductory phrase at 11:25 ("at that time") is repeated in 12:1. Rather than continuing with direct discourse, the narrator now tells the reader that the hungry disciples eat heads of grain on the Sabbath. The Pharisees object because they consider it work and, therefore, a violation of the law. Jesus responds with an extended statement. Notice that although the scene has shifted, the narrator continues to focus on Jesus' words rather than on his actions. Jesus' defense of his disciples is twofold: (1) they are hungry, just as David and his men were; and (2) it is no different from the work of the priests in the temple on the Sabbath. The implication is then explicitly drawn in 12:6: something greater than the temple is here.

Such a reaction verges on the satiric because of the introductory phrase: "Have you not read?" (12:3). If anyone in Palestine was intent on keeping the literal word of the Scriptures, it was the Pharisees; they have already (5:17-20) been presented as upholders of the tradition of the law. The rhetorical questions (12:3-5) and the sentence that follows (12:6), mentioning the temple, focus the reader's attention on the point the narrator intends to make: Jesus, the Son of God, overshadows the temple. This criticism is intensified in the next comment (12:7), which again belittles the opponents: "If you had known. . . ." The quotation is from Hos. 6:6 and again focuses on the temple and its limits. The disciples are guiltless because Jesus is present. It is not his status but the need for mercy that is crucial (cf. the Beatitudes, 5:2-11). Jesus concludes (12:8) with a statement about the Son of man and the Sabbath: as Lord of the Sabbath, his presence changes the context in which OT rules are understood. The narrator has already established that Jesus is the powerful Son of man, especially in the healing of the paralytic (8:20). If, then, the Son of man has the authority to forgive sins, the presence of the Son of man overrides the Pharisees' concern with the trivia of Sabbath regulations.

The impact of this incident, after the sayings in chap. 11, centers the reader's attention on the Pharisees' antagonism toward Jesus. Although the Pharisees are not directly addressed in 11:2-30, the implications for them are clear. Rather than warn or threaten them, as he warns the cities in 11:20-24, Jesus is described as presenting his argument with clarity and documentation. As the narrator has done already, Jesus himself refers to the OT: David, priestly temple activity, and Hosea; all these items demonstrate the close connection between Jesus and the narrator. The reader, who knows how much authority Jesus really has and who has just been reminded of Jesus' consciousness of his sonship, cannot miss the connection. If the "yoke" of 11:30 is the law, then 12:1–8 begins to explain what that "light and easy" yoke really is.

In 12:9–14 the narrator continues to focus on the Pharisees: they are the antecedent of "their" in the phrase "their synagogues" (12:9). Since it is still the Sabbath, "they" ask him directly if it is lawful to heal on the Sabbath. The narrator comments by telling the reader that their purpose was deceptive: to accuse him. Jesus' response to the direct question is to ask a rhetorical question about their own reasoning. Arguing from the lesser to the greater, Jesus rejects the implied criticism with an argument from experience rather than an OT quotation or an analogy about temple practice. Jesus is blunt this time: it is lawful to do good on the Sabbath, changing the Pharisees' "healing" to "do good." Then the healing miracle is reported shortly and quickly. The Pharisees, we are told, as a result of this double rebuff, conspire on "how to destroy him" (12:14). Thus the Pharisees have developed from calling Jesus crazy (9:34) to actively planning his destruction.

Matt. 12:14 is the first definite statement that the narrator has made about the Pharisees' antagonism. Jesus warned the disciples in chap. 10 about persecution; now we are informed that this antagonism has become a reality. It was hinted at earlier (chaps. 1 and 2); now Jesus' action and attitude have raised their ire. The narrator has encouraged the reader to sympathize with Jesus, especially with the quotation: "It is lawful to do good" (12:12).

JESUS' REACTION AND RATIONALE (12:15–21)

The narrator now interrupts the action at 12:15–21 to inform the reader that Jesus knew of their designs against him and, as a result, withdraws. Whether Jesus "knows" their thoughts in a magical sense or can surmise from their action and attitude, we are not told. But his response is to withdraw, unlike the previous reaction when he moved into their territory. He is followed by a crowd and he heals "all of them," perhaps in defiance of the Pharisees and their restrictive views. We are also informed that he did not want the healed followers to "make him known" (12:16). This will, of course, puzzle the reader because Jesus has been quite open about his healing and "unlawful" activity. This comment, which seems contradictory, forces the reader again to probe for some explanation—it is a gap that requires some filling. The problem for the reader is further complicated by the next statement, "This was to fulfill. . ." (12:17). The reader is already well acquainted with this phrase which shows God's control, influence, and guidance. A problem arises, however, in identifying the antecedent of "this." The Greek text reads simply "in order to fulfill the word . . ." or "so that the word was fulfilled . . ." the construction, ambiguous in Greek, seems to refer back to the previous clause, to the order for silence.

The quotation itself (12:18–21) is from Isa. 42:1–4, the longest and most complex quotation yet encountered in the story. Since it begins with the now familiar introduction about fulfillment, it reminds the reader once again of the Father's influence on Jesus' life. Silence is mentioned in v. 19. But the opening of the quotation reinforces another feature of the first chapters of the narrative: that God chose Jesus, gave him the Spirit at his baptism, and is pleased with him. This reminder of the opening framework is followed by an anticipation of the future with a reference to Gentiles being the object of his preaching, but it also recalls that in the infancy stories Gentiles are the first to worship him. This is further complicated by the fact that the disciples were told in chap. 10 not to go to the Gentiles; nonetheless, he is the hope of the Gentiles.

Placing this quotation in the midst of a concentrated attack on Jesus by the Pharisees enables the narrator to remind the reader of the overall context of the narrative; to recall the past, and to anticipate the future. There are other aspects of the quotation that will puzzle the reader and encourage hypothesis formation, especially the phrase, "until he brings justice to victory" (12:20). The plan is unfolding as the Father expected; the end result is certain to be what the Father planned. Despite the clouds that are now beginning to form, the future is assured. As yet, however, we have been given no clear hint about what it might be.

NEGATIVE REACTION CONTINUES (12:22–50)

Narration resumes again at 12:22, a typical healing incident; the crowd asks if this person could be the son of David, the one who heals. The Pharisees repeat their earlier accusation about the demonic source of Jesus' powers, a clear contrast to the positive reaction of the crowd. To reassert the power of Jesus, the narrator says that Jesus knew their thoughts, despite the fact that the Pharisees are reported to have *spoken* their accusation. Thus, Jesus' response is a direct reaction to the Pharisees' accusation and its negative implications.

In this confrontation (12:22–32) the son of David is contrasted to the servant or follower of Beelzebul. The narrator explained the connection to David in the genealogy (1:1–17), referring to Joseph as son of David. Similarly, we have been carefully prepared to suspect the Pharisees and their antagonism to Jesus. Thus, even though there are no value judgments explicitly expressed, the reader has no trouble identifying the narrator's stance. The apparently unnecessary "knowing their thoughts" functions in multiple ways.

Jesus' response is different from the *ad hominem* attack of the Pharisees. Instead, he seeks to demonstrate the illogical nature of their accusation; it is not typical in the world to undermine your own authority and power. He then concludes with a rhetorical question which indicates that the Pharisees themselves know the answer whether they will admit it or not (12:25–26). The Pharisees' next question (12:27) demonstrates their inconsistency and bias; they accept some exorcism but not from Jesus.

After criticizing the Pharisees by indirection, Jesus presses home his main point (12:28): he works in unity with the Spirit, as shown at the baptism and as stated in the quotation from Isaiah (12:18). And since this is the case, the conclusion is obvious: "the kingdom of God has come upon you" (12:28). This is the first time that the kingdom has been described as "of God" and probably because of the phrase "the Spirit of God" used earlier in the verse. The immediate context would lead the reader to think of the kingdom of God as the reign of the one who casts out demons and thus it answers the immediate problem, that is, that Jesus' power is from God, not from the devil. The healing activity of Jesus, and the disciples, is being underlined as especially significant even though the Pharisees disagree.

The following analogy (12:29) helps to clarify this point. By again resorting to a question, Jesus inquires how it is possible to burgle the house of a strong man without first controlling him. The reader is thus reminded of the temptations in Matthew 4 where Jesus meets and defeats the tempter. The conclusion is a statement: "Then he may plunder his house," as indeed Jesus is now doing.

The focus of the rest of the sayings (12:30–37) shifts to the contrast between those who are like the Pharisees and those who are like the disciples and followers. To be with Jesus is equivalent to being on God's side, to gather rather than to scatter (a reference to the harvest, as in chap. 10). The "therefore" of 12:31 signals a conclusion: the judgment will be based on one's response to Jesus. The narrator forces the reader to connect the two ideas—sin and blasphemy are equivalent to not "being with" Jesus. But the result is not always fatal; to blaspheme against the Spirit, that is, against the God who has given Jesus his authority and continues to guide him, is the truly fatal flaw. This is made more explicit by repeating in 12:32 the warning but substituting Son of man for the first (forgivable) sin, and changing Spirit to Holy Spirit. And the principle holds for every age. Thus, to attack Jesus as an individual is forgivable, but to question the source of his authority, his origins, is to deny God himself. This conclusion would not be unexpected for the reader, since in 11:25–30 the intimate connection between Father and Son was clearly stated. The reader gains a clear indication of how Jesus can counteract the antagonism of the Pharisees. They have revealed how truly perverse they are; they neither read the Scriptures nor do they think clearly and logically.

The last segment of the sayings (12:33–37) pushes home just this point. The analogy of the good tree and its good fruit was first introduced by John the Baptist in his attack on the Pharisees (3:8–10). It was also included in the Sermon on the Mount (7:15–20). Its inclusion here, complete with John's phrase "brood of vipers," is now directly aimed at the Pharisees' attack. They have illustrated where their sympathies lie, where their treasure is. They will be judged accordingly. Note that the threats in 12:31–32 and 12:36–37 are stated with future verbs; the Father's judgment in the future is certain.

The Pharisees are not convinced, however. The narrator tells us that they now ask to see a sign (12:38), addressing Jesus as "teacher." Despite the many signs or acts of power that Jesus has performed, these opponents want more. The reader can only wonder whether they have something more spectacular in mind or whether they are simply perverse and stubborn. The word sign has not appeared previously and could signal a request for something above and beyond the miracles already described. Jesus answers bluntly, using typically prophetic language, calling them an evil and adulterous generation. He refuses to give any sign "except the sign of the prophet Jonah," which is explained as his future death and subsequent return to life. The important point seems to be that the sign they demand *will* come but only in the future. A future sign, a promise, is not what they want. Thus the connection with the previous paragraph is now clear: a request for a sign is just another instance of how the scribes and Pharisees condemn themselves by their own words. And their condemnation is underlined by the double comparison that follows (12:41–42). The Ninevites who listened to Jonah "will" condemn those who do not listen to Jesus, the one who is greater than Jonah. Likewise with the Queen of the South: Jesus' wisdom is greater than Solomon's, whether the Pharisees acknowledge it or not.

This confrontation ends with the unusual story of the unclean spirit who, when evicted, returns with seven other evil spirits. In this context, especially with the preceding sayings about judgment, the reader will see the implied criticism of the Pharisees and scribes. Exorcism was mentioned at the beginning of the section (12:22). We must assume, then, that the forces of evil have taken over the Pharisees and scribes ("this evil generation"). The opposition to Jesus is identified with terms used at the temptation: the tempter is using his forces to influence even the "pillars" of the Jewish community. Finally, since the cleansed house is unoccupied by a good spirit, the evil spirits will return in increased numbers. The scribes and Pharisees are lost.

The narrator completes this section which documents the opposition to Jesus by reporting that Jesus' mother and brothers want to speak to him (12:46–50). They are "outside," even though it is not clear exactly where the preceding confrontation has taken place. His reply is unexpected: "Who is my mother and who are my brothers?" Such a question is, of course, ironic and the reader is being prepared to readjust his or her point of view. The narrator reports that Jesus, using a gesture of healing (stretching out his hand), declares that the *disciples* are his mother and brothers, that is, they do "the will of my Father in heaven." Thus, once again, the reader is reminded of the primary thrust of the narrative: Jesus is the Son and the Father's will is his guiding principle, controlling both his action and his assessment of people and events. Even family and kin must be redefined. We have already been advised of such a consequence in 10:21, but now it is portrayed in the narrative itself. On another level, however, the reader knows that Jesus' true father is the divine Father and, as a result, is partially prepared for the saying.

As the next incident shows, this is the conclusion of this subsection. By ending with a reference to the disciples, the narrator reinforces the contrast between the opponents and the disciples.

PARABLES FOR THE CROWD (13:1-32)

The change of location in 13:1-2 from house to sea and the change of audience from Pharisees to crowds signal to the reader a new phase in the story. Because the crowd is large, Jesus sits in a boat. In this way the narrator sets the scene for a major speech. He tells us that Jesus spoke in parables. Notice (1) that Jesus is not described as "teaching" and (2) that this is the first time the narrator has used the word "parable" (13:3).

The first story/parable (13:3-9) is about a sower and the fate of the seed; the fate is determined by the place the seed falls; the sequence is from no growth to full and complete growth. At the conclusion, Jesus implies that there is a lesson to be learned: "He who has ears, let him hear" (13:9). This same phrase appeared earlier when Jesus implied that John the Baptist was Elijah (11:15). So the reader is alerted that there is something more than usual being implied.

This second level of meaning is then directly stated, and the reader's anticipation is met, when in the next verse (13:10) the disciples ask Jesus why he speaks to the crowd in parables. It is significant that they do not ask him what this parable means, but rather why he uses *parables* when speaking to the crowd. The reader is thereby led to consider the distinction between the message to the crowds and the message to the disciples.

Jesus' response is direct. The disciples "have been given to know the secrets of the kingdom of heaven" (13:11) while the crowds have not. This declaration is followed by the aphoristic saying that those who have received will receive more, while those who have not, will receive nothing (13:12). The emphasis falls on the will of the Father and his Son who do what they wish, the theme that was stated in 11:25-27. The advantage that the disciples have is based on the Father's will and not on their own merit. Jesus then restates the theme and explains the mode of speaking in a different way, using words similar to Isaiah 6 about seeing and hearing.

This combination of items is the narrator's way of explaining how the reader should interpret the quotation: God has selected a group of disciples and gives them the capacity to understand. Because Jesus uses the formula quotation, it reinforces the reader's sense of (1) the continuity between Jesus and the Father, (2) God's careful control of all events, and (3) the reliability of the narrator. The word "secrets" in 13:11 occurs only here in Matthew but its association with the kingdom of heaven gives the reader a context. The contrast between the disciples and the crowd is stated in 13:16, when Jesus uses a beatitude to emphasize what the disciples have received: sight and hearing. In fact, they are more privileged than "many prophets and righteous men" (13:17) who have not had the same advantage.

Then in 13:18–23 Jesus explains the parable of the sower. If, indeed, the disciples are privileged to hear *and* understand, an explanation would be unnecessary. However, this is the narrator's way of including the reader in the company of the disciples. Verse 18 begins, "You then (will) hear" and functions as an explanation for the reader since we are very seldom told exactly what the disciples do understand. The seed is described as the "word of the kingdom" (a phrase unique to Matthew) but one which reinforces the heavy emphasis on the kingdom with which this section began; the secrets, then, are now being presented. The explanation is based on a parallel between soil and person. The seed is assumed to be constant; it is the soil that determines the outcome. The conclusion repeats a phrase we have heard before: the bearing of fruit. Understanding the word seems to mean more than an intellectual grasp of information. It should result in certain action, as was the point in the parable about the two houses (7:23–27) at the conclusion of the Sermon on the Mount.

After the explanation of the parable about the sower, the narrator seems to be deliberately ambiguous about Jesus' audience—the disciples or the crowd (13:24). When he says it was "put before" them, it refers back to the disciples but then in 13:34, the narrator clearly says he spoke to the crowds.

Unlike the first parable (13:3–9), each of these next three parables begins with (1) the narrator telling us directly that Jesus is speaking a "parable" and (2) Jesus speaking with the phrase "the kingdom of heaven is like. . . ." The emphasis on the kingdom of heaven continues as it began in 13:11, now explicitly mentioned so that the reader will not miss it.

The first of these parables, in 13:24–30, is again about seed, but now the problem is not the ground on which it falls, but on the kind of seed and on the distinction between the sowers. The point is: plants must grow to maturity before one can separate good from bad.

Another parable follows immediately (13:31–32), again with "a man" sowing seed. This time it is the *size* of the seed that is stressed: it is assumed that the seed is good and will produce a useful plant.

The next short parable (13:33) has a similar introduction. But in this case, it is not about seeds used for planting but about seeds used for food, namely, meal.

THE REASON FOR SPEAKING
IN PARABLES (13:34-35)

At this point (13:34) the narrator interrupts to remind the reader that Jesus spoke to the crowd *only* in parables. To reemphasize about the basic context for all Jesus' activity, that he is guided by God, we have another fulfillment quotation about parables and their potential for revealing what has always been hidden. Both the introduction and the quotation emphasize the divine purpose in Jesus' style of teaching. The reader's image of Jesus is further enhanced. The similarity between this passage and the statement of Jesus' authority in 11:25–27 and, second, the overarching impact of the heavenly Father carefully lead the reader.

PARABLES FOR THE DISCIPLES (13:36-52)

After this interruption of the plot, the narrator returns to the story by noting another change of location (13:36): leaving the crowds, Jesus enters "the house." When the disciples come to him again, as in 13:10, the crowds are not present; Jesus speaks to them privately. Their question this time is about the meaning of the parable of the weeds (13:24–30). Jesus' explanation (13:37–43) is allegorical, as was the explanation of the sower, but the good seeds now represent the "sons of the kingdom" not the "word." Also, emphasis is placed on the deceit of the "evil one" who scatters his "sons" in the world. The final judgment is especially prominent: the burning of weeds is contrasted to the gathering and storing of the wheat. The connection between the Son of man and the Father is also reinforced by mentioning the kingdom of the Father (13:43). The interpretation ends with the warning: "He who has ears, let him hear"—implying that further interpretation is necessary.

The narrator does not yet intervene: Jesus is reported to go on speaking—relating three more parables, without any interruption, as though they were all intended to give insight and understanding (secrets of the kingdom) to the disciples. Although these stories or analogies are not called parables, they all begin with the same opening phrase as that used earlier: "The kingdom of heaven is like. . . ." The two stories about finding treasure and a pearl (13:44–46) are not explained; the story about the sorting of many fish (13:47–50) repeats two phrases from the explanation of the parable of the weeds: (1) "so it will be at the close of the age" (13:49) and (2) "weeping and gnashing of teeth" (13:50). The image of burning is also repeated. The narrator is thereby encouraging the reader to see the connection between a judgment in the future and the fulfillment quotation that underlined the revealing of God's secrets. Part of the content of the secret, then, is the future judgment and the basis for the distinctions God makes at that time.

Finally this third major speech ends with a direct question to the disciples: "Have you understood all this?" The disciples answer, "Yes" (13:51).

This is a crucial point in the narrative, perhaps a turning point. Prior to this statement, the reader has been given very little help in deciding whether the disciples are reliable or not. We were informed about Jesus' attitude toward the disciples in 11:25–30, for example, and we have heard, at length, what Jesus expects of them. But we have not received much information about how they react, either directly from the narrator or in the narration. Thus the reader would be inclined to accept at face value the answer of these men who continue to follow Jesus; they probably do understand the kingdom of heaven. Their forthright answer is followed with a saying in which Jesus informs them of the direct consequences of their admission. The "therefore" in 13:52 implies that what follows is logically connected to their affirmative response. "Every scribe" would be a disciple (or someone in a similar situation) who has been trained for the kingdom of heaven, the obvious point of the previous speech. But Jesus goes on to tell them another parable, comparing the scribe to a householder and his treasure. It is appropriate that a "collection" of parables should end with a parable that implies that the reader must become like the disciples in order to understand the kingdom of heaven. The reader is drawn into the story, as a result, and is required to supply his own meaning. The clues we have been given about the householder are significant: in 10:25 a householder was called Beelzebul by his enemies, implying that Jesus is the householder; in 13:27 a householder is the figure with both authority and insight in the parable of the weeds. Here at the conclusion of the speech, a scribe is "like" a householder who. . . . The image is certainly a positive one; the metaphorical use of treasure in previous chapters would suggest, then, that the true disciple is one who uses both his own wisdom and the wisdom given to him. The narrator is anticipating a theme that will emerge fully in chap. 16.

THE RESPONSE OF HIS OWN COUNTRY (13:53-58)

For the third time we are confronted in 13:53 with the phrase that marks the end of a major speech. The narrator intervenes not only to tell us that this is the end but also to indicate a radical change of location: "He went away from there and (came) to his own country" (13:54). Jesus is said to have taught, we now know basically what he teaches, and "they" are astonished. The reasons for this astonishment are explained in the following quotation, a series of rhetorical questions about the source of Jesus' wisdom and mighty works. The reader is well aware of this problem which was clearly answered in 11:25-30. Thus the question format involves the reader by raising questions that he or she can indeed answer. Nevertheless, the attitude of the home-town folk is understandable.

Jesus' neighbors are scandalized (13:57) by him, an attitude Jesus had condemned (1) in 11:6 when he spoke about John the Baptist and (2) in 13:21, in the description of the seed that fell on rocky ground. Jesus reacts by quoting a proverb about a prophet lacking honor at home. This is the second implied reference to Jesus as prophet (10:41; 13:57) and it anticipates the fact that Jesus will be considered a prophet by some of the crowd.

The reference in 13:57 to lack of honor in both his own country and his own house is important. It ties this statement to the incident that preceded the parable speech (12:49-50, where disciples = family). The narrator implies, in addition, a connection between a prophet and mighty works by explaining the scarcity of mighty works "because of their unbelief" (13:58). "Unbelief" occurs only here in the narrative, although a similar word (faithless) occurs in 17:17. In this context, it means that the home-town people do not recognize the origin of his teaching and miracles. Their faults are obvious to the reader.

HEROD'S RESPONSE (14:1-12)

The next paragraph begins (14:1) with a time reference ("at that time") but Herod is now the subject; Herod the Tetrarch, the narrator tells us, distinguishing him from his famous father mentioned in the birth story. Since Jesus is in Galilee, it is Herod Antipas who is intended. We were told in 4:24 that Jesus' fame spread throughout all Syria and now we hear that Herod is beginning to take notice. The narrator informs us, using direct quotation, that Herod is worried about Jesus because he thinks John the Baptist has returned from the dead. Why a king should be concerned about a religious teacher such as Jesus is left unexplained; it is the death of John, which has not even been mentioned before, that the narrator wants to highlight. As a result, a flashback is required because he died sometime between the present moment in the narrative and the events narrated in chap. 11, when John the Baptist was still alive in prison. This is the only time the narrative does not parallel the story; the narrator consciously delays reporting this incident until it is important for his story. Since Herod does not appear elsewhere, but John the Baptist has been prominently featured, it is a way of giving the reader specific information about John the Baptist and his relation to Jesus.

Herod Antipas is pictured as a superstitious individual who acts primarily on impulse. Notice that the narrator is privy to much "inside" information; he knows, for example, that Herod had been annoyed by John's criticism of his adulterous relations with his brother Phillip's wife. Herod, who had already imprisoned John the Baptist, kills him after making a rash promise while drunk; he would rather destroy John than be embarrassed in front of the "company" by refusing to carry out his promise. The real villain is Herodias, portrayed as vindictive and overbearing. We are told that Herod is "sorry" but he is, nonetheless, willing to do as Herodias requests. The narrator makes the connection with the preceding material, however, when he mentions that Herod was reluctant to act against John because the people considered him a prophet. So Herod is clearly manipulated by the opinion of others. Thus, with this grisly story, the narrator reminds the reader, once more, of the similarity between John the Baptist and Jesus.

THE RESPONSE CONTINUES (14:13–36)

The purpose of the flashback is clear in the next paragraph (14:13–21). Jesus hears about "this," that is, he hears that Herod thinks he is John the Baptist raised from the dead. Jesus then withdraws. Thus the reader sees Jesus trying to avoid a confrontation with the political authorities, apparently because of Herod's recent willingness to act against a prophet. The ruler of "his country" is a potential enemy. However, Jesus' fame is such that the crowds continue to follow him; he does what he had previously done, but now in a "lonely place" (14:13). The narrator makes it clear that Jesus is pursued relentlessly by the crowds; he cannot get away from them even though he goes some distance by boat. In a rare instance of omniscience, the narrator reports that Jesus healed "their sick" because he had compassion on them (14:14). The same motive was reported in 9:36 just prior to the mission speech. It will influence the reader, of course, appearing just after the story of Herod's strange motives and the danger that Jesus perceived and yet ignored. It also helps to establish the context for the following event, the miraculous feeding; miracles of healing and feeding both result from Jesus' compassion.

Compassion is also prominent in 14:15 when the narrator implies that the disciples are concerned for the people. They are quoted as suggesting that Jesus send the crowds away to purchase food. When Jesus tells them to feed the crowd themselves (14:16), they reply that they have only very limited supplies (14:17). The rest of the paragraph (14:19–21) is narration; the narrator tells us that Jesus first looked up into heaven as he blessed the loaves; then the disciples distribute the food; the entire crowd is satisfied; and twelve baskets of food remain. The size of the crowd is mentioned at the end, creating a bit more tension and heightening the effect on the reader. Jesus' compassion, authorized by the Father in heaven, is thoroughly documented.

In 14:22 the narrator moves the focus back to the disciples, mentioning their departure before noting that the crowd is dismissed. Jesus retreats into the hills to pray. Notice that the narrator links the isolation of Jesus with the report of the disciples' situation out on the lake: they are far from the land and are having a difficult time making their way to "the other side." We are abruptly informed, then, that Jesus comes to them walking on the sea (14:25). The reader must assume that Jesus is aware of their need and comes, perhaps again out of compassion, although his motives are not stated. Since it is near morning, their progress across the lake has indeed been slow. The narrator states quite simply that Jesus walks on the sea. The reader is by now accustomed to Jesus' miraculous actions, knowing his origins, but the disciples are troubled; they are quoted as saying, "It is a ghost" ("appearance" or "apparition") and we are told they cry out for fear (14:26). It is interesting to note that the disciples do not realize who it is, that Jesus must identify himself. The imperative "Take heart" is a phrase also used twice before, always in connection with a miracle. It implies that they should be bold or confident; and Jesus adds, "Have no fear."

Rather than tell us how the disciples respond, the narrator quotes Peter (14:28) who says, "Allow me to *come to you.*" After the narrator describes Peter's success in walking on the sea, he mentions his fear when he sees the wind. As he sinks, Peter cries, "Lord, save me." This plea is similar to the prayer uttered by the disciples at the stilling of the storm (8:25). As Jesus reaches for him, he says, "O man of little faith, why did you doubt?" (14:31). We have encountered the words "little faith" twice before, the first time in the Sermon on the Mount (6:30) when Jesus chastises those who are anxious about clothing. The second was at the stilling of the storm when the anxiety of the disciples was the issue, and where the word "save" was also used (8:18–27). This clustering of terms is significant and would affect the reader's grasp of the developing portrait of the disciples. In each case notice that it is a phrase used by Jesus, not an opinion of the narrator. The word "doubt" implies that they are uncertain ("of two minds") rather than incredulous.

When the wind ceased, as Jesus and Peter got into the boat, the narrator tells us that those in the boat worshiped him, saying, "Truly you are the Son of God" (14:33). The word for "truly" is best translated as "certainly" and is a different word from the one that the narrator uses at the beginning of some of Jesus' sayings, that is, *Amen*. The main point of this incident, of course, is the disciples' confession that Jesus is the Son of God. Earlier in the story, the narrator referred to Jesus as Son (of God) in a fulfillment quotation (2:15), God called him "my Son" at the baptism (3:17), the devil taunted him with the title twice in the temptation (4:3, 6), and two demoniacs call him Son of God (8:26). Thus it is significant that *the disciples* call him Son of God. The reader, knowing Jesus' origins, has been led by the narrator to acknowledge this fact from the beginning of the story. But now the disciples are shown to finally see what should have been clear to them earlier. The saying in 11:25–30 should have prepared them for this insight, although there was some ambiguity about whether they were present at that time.

As if to underline this recognition, the next paragraph (14:34–36) reports the landing in Gennesaret, in Jesus' own territory close to Capernaum, where the people bring again their sick, as the narrator says, to merely touch the fringe of his garment. This act, says the narrator, resulted in healing for anyone who did indeed touch it. Such a statement is another instance of the crowd being described as having a faith close to the faith of the disciples; they are not antagonistic.

OPPOSITION RESUMES (15:1–9)

The positive portrait of the crowd is contrasted, however, in 15:1–

9, with the Pharisees. They come with a question about the disciples' lack of adherence to the laws of cleanliness. Although there is no change of location, that is, Jesus is still apparently in Gennesaret, we are told that the Pharisees and scribes came from Jerusalem. The Pharisees mentioned previously were never identified in any other way, thus the description "from Jerusalem" introduces a theme absent since the opening narratives. Jesus' response is to support his disciples indirectly; he asks why these Pharisees and scribes from Jerusalem transgress the command of God, thereby highlighting the distinction between the tradition of the elders (followed by the Pharisees and scribes) and the command of God.

God commanded, says Jesus, and quotes Exod. 20:12, 17; Lev. 20:9, and Deut. 5:16. When Jesus says "but you say" (15:5), the reader is reminded of the antitheses in Matthew 5 and forced to think about the difference between Jesus' interpretation of the OT and that of his critics. Jesus says that they have "made void" the word of God, which is, of course, in direct contrast to Jesus' claim that he fulfills the Scripture. They are hypocrites, says Jesus. This is a term that has not been used since the Sermon on the Mount (6:2, 5, 16; 7:5) where it was associated with false piety and self-satisfaction. The point here is similar. The Pharisees and Sadducees are accused of using one facet of the law, giving goods or money to God, in order to avoid another requirement, the support of one's parents. This, however, is the first time that the reader is informed of the identity of the hypocrites. The opposition to Jesus is now explicitly identified as the Pharisees and Sadducees, especially those who come from Jerusalem. The confrontation is further intensified when Jesus quotes from Isaiah saying that Isaiah's condemnation of those who misrepresent God is applicable to these opponents. There is also a reminder here of the criticism of chap. 13 in the reference to the hearts of these hypocrites.

THE IMPORTANCE OF
UNDERSTANDING (15:10—16:12)

The importance of understanding is also emphasized by the narrator: he reports that Jesus turns away from the Pharisees and Sadducees, calls the people to him, and prefaces his teaching with the exhortation to hear and understand. The saying itself is short and to the point: what defiles is what comes out of a person and not what goes into him. The disciples, over whose actions this exchange was initiated, now are reported to ask Jesus if he realizes that the

Pharisees were offended. Apparently we are to assume that they respect these leaders. But Jesus continues to speak parabolically: what God did not plant will be rooted up, a clear reference to the parable of the weeds (13:24–30) with the additional implication about the source of the Pharisees' thoughts. Jesus says they should be avoided. They are blind guides; when the blind lead the blind, disaster results. The direct admonition to the disciples ("Let them alone") between images has the added effect of forcing the reader to apply these sayings to the immediate situation.

When Peter responds by asking for an explanation (15:15), the reader is inclined to wonder why he doesn't comprehend. The disciples were supposed to have received the capacity to understand the parables (13:11), and they have been instructed often. But now they show a lack of comprehension. Jesus responds first by asking two questions, heightening the tension. "Are you without understanding? Don't you know (or see)?" He then proceeds to explain the importance of the heart as a source of action. The evil thoughts are listed (15:16–20).

As a result of this confrontation, the reader's view of the disciples is ambivalent. Jesus defends them against the accusations of the Pharisees and Sadducees but they have demonstrated that they are slow to comprehend. They continue to need instruction and guidance.

The narrator notes a change in Jesus' location. He withdraws to the northwest, to the region of Tyre and Sidon. If it is because of the Pharisees and Sadducees, we are not told; it *is* a move away from Jerusalem. We *are* told that a non-Israelite woman came and appealed to Jesus; addressing him as Lord and Son of David, she asks for mercy, announcing that her daughter is possessed of a demon. The narrator reports that Jesus says nothing; the disciples, however, ask Jesus to send her away. He tells the *disciples* that he is sent only to the lost sheep of the house of Israel.

This is the second incident in which a Gentile approaches Jesus for help. The Centurion of Capernaum (8:5–13) asked for help, acknowledged Jesus' authority, and was sensitive enough to Jewish purity laws to avoid asking Jesus to violate them. Here in chap. 15, however, Jesus is traveling in non-Jewish territory, apparently to get away from the Pharisees and Sadducees. Consequently, his response to the disciples (15:24) is not clear, except perhaps to remind them that he is not here in gentile territory for "missionary" purposes.

When the Canaanite woman persists, he speaks directly to her using parabolic language, "It is not fair to take children's bread and throw it to dogs" (15:26,. Her answer, using the same imagery, indicates that she knows what he intended and that she nonetheless requests help. Jesus' stonishing answer is: "Great is your faith," a phrase unique to this story, "be it done for you as you desire." The narrator adds that the daughter was healed instantly. Thus in the context, the reader will contrast the understanding exhibited by this Gentile with the perversity of the Pharisees and Sadducees and the dullness of the disciples. Unlike the incident with the Centurion, the focus is not on Jesus' authority, but on the woman's ability to understand Jesus' elliptical teaching (in addition to recognizing his power). The narrator made it prominent by noting the change in location, a change that is emphasized when, at the conclusion, the scene shifts back to Galilee (15:29–31). We are told that even though he continued to avoid every village or town, the crowds follow. This entire paragraph (vv. 29–31) is reported narrative and includes a narrator's statement about the "wondering" of the crowd as Jesus heals. In the last line, the narrator says they "glorify" the God of Israel. Thus the "lost sheep of the house of Israel" are repeatedly helped by Jesus, as he said he must in 15:24. The narrator is also reminding the reader of the control that God exercises over this whole story when the crowd glorifies not Jesus but God who sent him. The crowd understands the source of his authority, as the Canaanite woman did, and as the Pharisees and Sadducees do not.

With the crowds now the center of attention, Jesus is reported to summon the disciples and to express his compassion because of their (the crowd's) lack of food. On previous occasions, the narrator has ascribed this compassion to Jesus; here Jesus himself states it to the disciples (thereby verifying the reliability of the narrator, if such is still necessary). At the previous feeding story (14:13–21) the situation was less drastic; there was apparently food available but Jesus said they did not need to go away. In this instance, the desert setting is mentioned and the disciples ask specifically where they can find enough food. Seven loaves and a few fish are available. The rest of the incident is all narrated: the blessing and the breaking, the distribution by the disciples, the remaining seven baskets, and the number of the crowd (four thousand). The narrator does not indicate any reaction to the miracle. He merely says that Jesus sent them away and then moves back across the lake to Magadan. Since both feedings are prefaced with a reference to Jesus' compassion for the crowds, the reader is encouraged to view these miracles as specific acts of compassion, thus creating a very positive view of the crowd. Whether he intends any irony about the lack of understanding on the part of the disciples is not clear. The close proximity of the feedings would tend to point to this as another instance of the dullness, but not stupidity, of the followers.

The next incident (16:1) reports that the Pharisees, again accompanied by the Sadducees, confront Jesus. But the narrator now informs us that they come explicitly "to test him" by requesting a sign from heaven. This is the second time such a request has been made; in 12:38–42 Jesus refused "except for the sign of the prophet Jonah." Now they want a sign *from heaven,* says the narrator. Jesus' answer is, first, a quotation of a proverb about weather prediction, that is, a sign in the heavens. The whole passage could be interpreted as a play on the word "heaven-sky." Jesus changes the content of the saying by accusing the Pharisees of not paying attention to the "signs of the times" and concludes by repeating an accusation from the previous incident, that is, calling them an evil and adulterous generation, and reaffirming that a sign *will* be given, the sign of Jonah. The reader already knows that the sign of Jonah is the death and return of Jesus, a decisive event of the future. The narrator has demonstrated often enough that miracles are not uncommon when Jesus is present and the reader knows already (12:14) that the Pharisees have conspired to find a way to destroy him. When the narrator concludes by reporting simply that Jesus left them and went elsewhere, they are, in effect, given no chance to respond, and the reader is left with the impression that Jesus is shunning them.

The scene shifts (16:5) to the disciples and continues the story that ended at 15:39, giving the impression that 16:1–4 is an interruption, and further supporting the reader's impression about Jesus' shunning of the Pharisees. The narrator reports that the disciples had forgotten to bring any bread, presumably some of the leftovers from the feeding of the four thousand. Why they would need to do this is left unsaid. But, this apparent difficulty is solved when the narrator reports that Jesus says, "Take heed and beware of the leaven of the Pharisees and Sadducees." Thus the feeding (15:32–39) and the Pharisees' question, that is, the last two pericopes, are being interrelated. The disciples respond, we are told, by discussing it among themselves, saying, "We brought no bread." Now the initial sentence makes some sense. The narrator has anticipated this response so that when *we* read it, we see that they are thinking literally and have not understood the parabolic character of Jesus' saying, despite the fact that they should (cf. chap. 13). It is not clear whether the disciples heard the previous conversation; they could have crossed the lake separately. But the reader is encouraged to evaluate the disciples.

Jesus, aware of their uncertainty, says the narrator, asks why they are discussing his warning, calling them "those of little faith." This is the fourth and last time this epithet is used. In addition to indicating that Jesus knows the content of their private conversation, it reinforces the emphasis on the bread. Jesus continues, "Do you not yet perceive?" (16:9). The word "perceive" was used in 15:17 where, in a similar situation, Jesus asked why the disciples did not perceive the meaning of an analogy, the distinction between defilement by eating and speaking. Here in 16:8 Jesus asks a series of questions about the two feedings which ends by repeating the original saying about leaven. The implication is that if Jesus asks them the right questions, they will know the answer. He asks, "How is it that you fail to perceive that I did not speak about bread? Beware of the leaven of the Pharisees and Sadducees." Thus without actually explaining what he means by the leaven, Jesus is portrayed as reminding the disciples, by indirection, what they should have understood. The narrator closes the paragraph (16:12) by telling the reader that the disciples *then* understood that Jesus was warning them about the teaching of the Pharisees and Sadducees. The reader is therefore encouraged to think more highly of the disciples because they have, perhaps, made some progress. At the same time this section increases the reader's apprehension about the Pharisees and Sadducees. The reader is also encouraged to be aware of the parabolic nature of Jesus' sayings and to look for a deeper meaning. The disciples and the reader should be able to understand what Jesus is doing. Thus the ordering of events and the mode of presentation have brought the reader closer to the disciples.

PETER CONFESSES (16:13–20)

The narrator now reports a more extensive change in location—to Caesarea Philippi. This is the only time Jesus goes very far beyond Galilee and the only time he goes in this direction, to the north. Previously, any departure from Galilee resulted in contact with non-Jews. This time it is different: Jesus asks his disciples, "Who do men say that the Son of man is?" The reader knows that Jesus is the Son of man and also his origins and abilities. In addition, we have just been told that the disciples understood his teaching about the Pharisees and Sadducees. In answer they report what others are saying: Jesus is

John the Baptist, Elijah, Jeremiah, or one of the pֶrֵoֶpֶhֶeֶtֶs. When asked *their* opinion, Peter responds, "You are the Christ (Messiah), the Son of the living God." This is the second time the disciples have acknowledged Jesus' origins; the first time was after he walked on the sea (14:22–33). In both cases, Peter is presented either as a spokesman or as a representative. The new feature here, of course, is the title "Christ." The narrator has not used this title since (1) the opening scenes (chaps. 1 and 2) and (2) the isolated reference to "the deeds of the Christ" in 11:2. The reader, therefore, would not be surprised at this response and is encouraged to recognize the disciples' improving insight and understanding.

The statement made by Jesus in 16:17–20 reminds the reader of the overall and commanding perspective of the story, that God is in full control.

Notice that Simon is called "Son of Jonah" (unique to this passage) and he is declared "blessed." This word was used in 5:3–12 to set the theme of Jesus' ministry at the opening of the Sermon on the Mount (the Beatitudes), in 11:6 to describe the person who is not scandalized, and in 13:16 to describe the disciples who were privileged to hear and see the teaching and deeds of Jesus. But, Jesus adds, the reason for the blessing is the fact that Peter does not speak on his own; rather he speaks as a prophet who received this revelation from the "Father who is in heaven." Because he speaks as a prophet, he is given the nickname "Rock," for it is on him that Jesus will found his church against which the powers of death will not prevail. Thus the words of Jesus continue to focus on the cosmic dimension of the conflict. Finally, Jesus promises to give Peter the keys of the kingdom of heaven, that is, the responsibility for binding and loosing on earth. The authority with which Jesus speaks reminds us of the earlier assertion about the intimate relation between Jesus and the Father (11:25–30), although the image of keys and loosing-binding is new. The narrator ends this incident by reporting that Jesus "strictly" charged them to tell no one that he was the Christ; it reminds the reader of the import of this section, that is, that the disciples, with God's assistance, recognize him as Messiah, a fact the reader has known from the beginning of the narrative.

THE DISCIPLES ARE INSTRUCTED (16:21—17:27)

In 16:21 the narrator appears to change the time scale: "from that time" implies repeated action into the future. "Jesus began to show them that he must go to Jerusalem and suffer, be killed, and be raised." It is significant that these sayings are not described as teaching. When the narrator reports in 16:22 that Peter rebuked him, the reader can appreciate Peter's response. Jesus' death, although mentioned before (12:14, 40) would seem rather unlikely, given the power he has displayed, not to mention the authority and support Jesus has received from the Father. The narrator says first that Peter rebuked him and then quotes Peter: "God forbid, Lord. This shall never happen to you." Literally the Greek reads, "Gracious to you, Lord. This thing will not be to you," which appears to mean: Certainly God will be gracious to you, Lord, and not let this happen to you. Thus, in a way, Peter confirms what he has already confessed, that Jesus is God's son. He is presumptuous, however, in assuming that he knows God's will or plan. This reaction is, of course, consistent with what we have learned of Peter in chap. 14 when he walked on the water. Jesus' response to this outburst of piety is also unexpected because he addresses Peter as Satan, saying, "You are a hindrance to me" (16:23). The reader will recall the temptation in chap. 4; Jesus had resisted the tempter there and continues to do so here.

The point that the narrator has established, then, is not so much the instability of Peter but the way in which Jesus perceives the overall situation. Peter, influenced by God in 16:17, is controlled by Satan in 16:22. The disciples are involved in a conflict that transcends their own lives. Jesus is God's Son (11:25–30) who is waging a battle that is more extensive than it appears to the disciples, a battle against the forces of evil and Satan himself. The ultimate goal is the righteousness of the people; the conflict is defined by Satan's influence over people. Thus the statement in 16:12 about the source of the disciples' understanding establishes their inability to determine the outcome of the conflict on their own. The following incident (16:24–28), reported by the narrator, records Jesus' words to his disciples, trying to influence them once again. We were told that these Twelve *did* follow Jesus this far in the story; now they (and we) are warned about some of the risks, possibly the cross. Since we are fully convinced of Jesus' authority we must accept his evaluation of life. Especially powerful are the rhetorical questions in this context. Referring to himself as the Son of man and reaffirming his connection with the Father, he points ahead to the final accounting in the future. And as this reaffirmation concludes, he predicts that some of the disciples, despite what has just happened, will not die before he comes "in his kingdom."

With another time notation ("after six days") we are told that Jesus takes Peter, James, and John (the only time these three are singled out as a group) up onto a mountain where he is transfigured, a phenomenon described primarily in terms associated with light. Notice that the narrator shifts the point of view slightly by saying that Moses and Elijah appeared *to them,* as though this was being told as a report from their point of view, not from the narrator's noninvolved stance.

Peter speaks once again, as he had in 14:28, but this time there is no response from Jesus nor any comment by the narrator about his words. His offer to build three booths is probably a recognition of the presence of the Holy that he has just witnessed. But Peter is quoted as saying, "If you wish," which makes the lack of a reply from Jesus that much more significant. The reader must wonder if this, then, is another example of Peter speaking under the influence of God or Satan. The narrator proceeds to make it quite clear that Peter is once again speaking out of turn (as Satan?) when he reports that a bright cloud overshadowed them and that a voice speaks from it, that is, God himself speaks, interrupting Peter. God announces to the three disciples that Jesus is "my beloved Son, with whom I am well pleased; listen to him." The concluding admonition is an addition to the similar saying reported at the baptism. The implication is that Peter does not listen; it is another rebuke. The narrator reports that the three fell on their faces and were filled with awe (Greek = were very afraid). Then Jesus comes, touches them (a healing gesture), and tells them to rise and "have no fear," a phrase also associated with the walking on the sea in 14:27. Finally, the narrator tells us that when they look up they see only Jesus. Thus the scene is partially told from the disciples' point of view rather than just reporting that Jesus is alone or that Moses and Elijah are no longer present. The effect, of course, is to solidify the even closer connection between the reader and the disciples.

The importance of the mountain is stressed in the following paragraph (17:9–13) when the narrator mentions that they were "descending." Jesus "commands" them (a word used only sparingly in this story and often for God's demands): "Tell no one the vision, until the Son of man is raised." The word "vision" is unique; it tends to focus the reader's attention on the disciples' own involvement. The significance of the section is indicated by a second mention of Jesus' resurrection (16:21). The reader is encouraged to adjust to the idea of the death/resurrection as a part of God's plan for his beloved son. The disciples are then said to respond by asking about Elijah. Since they have just seen Elijah in the vision, we must assume that they are puzzled about the relationship between Jesus and Elijah. They now have even more reason to accept Jesus as the Messiah and, since they know that the scribes say that Elijah must come first, they ask an appropriate question. Jesus tells them that Elijah has already come and because "they" did not know him, he was persecuted. "So the Son of man will suffer at their hands." The context, then, makes it clear that "they" refers to Jesus' opponents who earlier said they would persecute him (elders, chief priests, and scribes, 16:21). To insure that the reader recognizes the reference, the narrator adds that "then" the disciples understood he was speaking about John the Baptist. The word "to understand," used in connection with the disciples before, creates a good impression on the reader. To understand Jesus is to comprehend a hidden or symbolic meaning. So the narrator (1) makes certain that the reader understands Jesus' reference, (2) improves the evaluation of the disciples, and (3) continues to develop the concept of suffering in connection with the title "Son of Man." Since John the Baptist died at the hands of Herod, it would be natural for the reader to associate the ruling authorities with the religious establishment—as was implied in chaps. 1 and 2.

Now that they have completed the descent of the mountain, a "man" speaks to Jesus, kneeling and calling him Lord (17:14–21). He is quoted as saying that his epileptic son could not be healed by the other nine disciples. So, while the select three were gaining insight and understanding, the remaining nine, or perhaps more, were demonstrating their insufficient faith. Jesus speaks to the disciples, not to the man, calling them a "faithless and perverse generation," a phrase that occurs only here in Matthew. His rebuke takes the form of two questions: "How long will I be with you?" and "How long will I put up with you?" This note of exasperation is intensified by the curt command: "Bring him here." The narrator tells us, then, that the boy was cured immediately when the demon was rebuked. The verb "rebuke" is used once again in close proximity to its use in 16:22 (where Peter rebukes Jesus and is then rebuked by Jesus in return). The narrator's interest in the incident is obvious when he concludes it with no reference to the father or to the cured boy but rather with a report of the private conversation of Jesus with his disciples. They inquire about their lack of ability and Jesus replies, "because of your little faith," followed by the assertion that even faith as small as a mustard seed would enable one to move a mountain. He finishes with the extravagant assertion that nothing is impossible. Thus Jesus is portrayed as a leader who continues to have great expectations for his followers and yet is disturbed by their inability to produce results.

As an introduction to the next saying, the narrator tells us that Jesus spoke as "they" were gathering in Galilee, giving the impression of a summary or conclusion (17:22–23). Jesus' words repeat the prediction that the Son of man will suffer and die. In the Greek, the word order stresses the nearness of the action, encouraging the reader to anticipate the coming difficulties. The disciples' reaction is reported: they were *very* distressed. The implication, of course, is that they recognize the seriousness and truth of the prediction. Thus the "training" of the disciples seems to have made significant progress, despite the setbacks or lapses, illustrated in the immediately preceding story. In effect, they are now doing what God required in 17:5, listening to the beloved Son.

The next incident (17:24–27) breaks a pattern. The reader expects once again to be told of a conflict between Jesus and the authorities but the narrator reports that the Jewish tax collectors ask *Peter* if Jesus pays the tax. Peter says, "Yes." The narrator implies that Jesus was not present at the time and that he "heard" about it some other way. In any case, Jesus initiates the ensuing conversation when Peter comes "into the house." This is the first time Jesus has asked anyone about what they "think." The three questions are really only one question with an option, about the taxing practices of "the kings of the earth." In reply Peter says that kings do not normally tax their own sons, they tax others. Jesus then draws the conclusion about the sons: since they are not usually taxed, they are free. The implication, in the light of the following instruction about finding the shekel and giving it in payment for both Peter and himself, is that the Pharisees' initial question was not to find out if Jesus ever paid but whether he will pay now. So, Jesus' reply indicates that he understands their question as a criticism that is invalid. But it is not worth insisting on, since the tax collectors do not recognize that Jesus and the disciples have any special status. The rationale for paying, then, is to avoid a scandal. This is an interesting distinction, since Jesus has previously said that his presence does indeed cause a scandal. Therefore, the reader will assume that the payment of the temple tax is not a crucial issue. Of course it is "solved" in a peculiar way, by the miraculous discovery of a shekel in a fish's mouth. Although it is not reported that Peter actually does find the shekel, the reader has every reason to assume that Jesus' expectation will be fulfilled, that God will arrange this as he has already supported Jesus in other ways.

Thus, after a summary statement about his death, this incident makes clear that Jesus and the disciples will not be sidetracked by such a minor scandal. The major issue is the cross.

ADVICE FOR THE COMMUNITY (18:1–35)

Having called Peter and, by implication, the other followers "sons," the narrator reports that the disciples came to Jesus and asked about their relative status in the kingdom. Their confidence about their acceptance is obvious. Except for the statement in 16:19, "the keys of the kingdom," the phrase "kingdom of heaven" has not been mentioned since the disciples were told the extended series of parables about the kingdom, which they said they understood. Peter was singled out as the recipient of the keys in 16:19 and here in 18:1 he is prominent again (although it is the disciples as a group that ask this question). The reader is thus encouraged to think in terms of the citizens of the kingdom and their responsibility in it.

The narrator's return to the subject of the kingdom continues as Jesus answers the question. We are first told that Jesus summoned a child to serve as an example for his teaching; he answers the question about rank by telling the disciples that they must "turn" and become like children to even *enter* the kingdom of heaven. The humbleness of the child is the point of comparison, he says, which leads to high status in the kingdom. Thus, the overconfidence of the disciples is again rejected. Jesus, however, changes the emphasis from the disciples to those who receive the disciples; the phrases "one such child" and "one of these little ones who believe in me" are references to the disciple who turns and becomes humble. Causing a little one to stumble results in direct punishment, although the punishment is only implied. The threat involved in the construction "it would be better" was already used twice before in the Sermon on the Mount (5:29–35). The implication, of course, is that God himself will deal with such a person and that this action leads to destruction or rejection. Thus, from a question about greatness in the kingdom of heaven, the narrator has explained the importance of humbleness, both for those wishing to enter the kingdom and for those who receive the "little ones" who come in his name. The narrator wants us to consider both the disciples and the wider community of followers. This double emphasis is reminiscent of the sayings in chap. 10 about the mission. The woe which follows (18:7) is intended for those in the world who do not accept his followers, despite the fact that their rejection is inevitable. But the main point is not to castigate those who persecute; rather, it is to offer encouragement to the disciples. The shift to second person singular in 18:8 heightens the force of the saying: the general nature of the earlier statements is reversed, although the transition is not clear. The woe is directed to "the person" who tempts, but now the temptation is said to come from one's own foot, hand, or eye. The terminology is, again, reminiscent of the Sermon on the Mount (5:29–30) which used the same extreme imagery about removing an eye or hand; in both cases the alternative is fire and hell.

This focus on the attitude of the followers is supplemented in 18:10 with eschatological terminology. To despise a humble one is tantamount to rejecting Jesus, in whose name they come. The angels are face to face with the Father in heaven who is, of course, in control of what transpires on the earth. The point is illustrated with a parable, introduced (18:12) by the direct challenge to interpret, that is, "What do you think?" (as in 17:25). The story of the shepherd who leaves ninety-nine sheep to seek the one who is lost closes with a direct application: the will of the Father is that the "little one" should be protected (18:14).

This sequence of sayings, then, is unified by the repeated use of the phrase "My Father who is in heaven." It is part of the technique the narrator has employed right from the start. The kingdom of heaven, the Father's realm, will be populated by humble ones, or little ones, who are sought by the Father. The greatest in the kingdom is the humble one; those who are not humble are punished.

The speech continues (18:15–20) with Jesus turning to a practical instance of how this humbleness is put to work; an offender deserves your solicitation; *you* should go to him, repeatedly, to seek his return. Only if he is adamant in his refusal is he to be condemned. This example is followed by a series of phrases that were used in chap. 16, addressed to Peter. Binding and loosing, in this context, result from acting on behalf of others, from attempting to bring them back into the fold. The point is reemphasized when Jesus says, "Again I say to you." The disciple should not act on his own; two must agree and if they do, God will support them. "For where two or three are gathered in my name, there am I in the midst of them" (18:20). The two or three are humble ones. The reader is therefore reminded of the opening section where receiving one person in Jesus' name means receiving

Jesus. The connection between Father and Son is certain: a repeat of the statement in 11:25–27. It is repeated here in a number of ways. The narrator told us initially that the child was placed in the midst of the disciples; now Jesus says *he* is in their midst if they gather in his name.

The continuity of the speech is interrupted at 18:21 when Peter asks about the numerical limits of forgiveness: is it seven times? Jesus' reply is extreme; you must forgive seventy times seven. If the limit is this high, condemnation is virtually impossible. *God* will condemn if he must. The connection with the previous saying is now clear; if Peter and the community are to bind and loose, then there is no practical limit to forgiveness. Jesus' reply says that the function of binding (or condemning) will be seldom used.

The subject is developed further with a parable, a long story about an unforgiving servant (18:23–35). Humility, required for entrance into the kingdom of heaven, is dramatically displayed. After being forgiven a huge debt owed to his master, the servant refuses to forgive a much smaller debt owed to him by a fellow servant. Both of the debtors in Jesus' story make the same appeal for patience and the same promise to pay eventually. The master is angered by the unforgiving servant's arrogance and throws him in jail. Jesus' concluding comment draws the implication: My Father will do the same to you if you do not forgive from your heart.

In this speech, the narrator has portrayed Jesus as a sensitive teacher who defines the character of the new community with family imagery. Beginning with a child, described as humble, the narrator next mentions the "little ones," changes the image to "brother," and then ends with the word "brother." There is also an emphasis on the future, when the Father will either reward or punish. The impression left with the reader after following this lengthy speech is that Jesus expects humility, manifested in a willingness to forgive.

5

The Message of the Kingdom Presented in Judea

19:1—25:46

Matthew 19 begins with the formula that marks the end of the five major speeches. The narrator tells us that Jesus leaves Galilee and enters the "region of Judea beyond the Jordan." This is a noteworthy change of location; Judea hasn't been mentioned since chaps. 2–4. It is the place of Jesus' birth (and the persecution by Herod the Great) and the home of some of the crowd that surrounds Jesus at the beginning of his ministry. In addition, the summary statement in 4:23–25 mentions both Judea and the area beyond the Jordan. Therefore this notice, at the beginning of chap. 19, is an indication of a new phase of the story. The crowds are still following Jesus and once again Jesus' healing is reported.

THE OPPONENTS ATTACK (19:3–22)

The first incident in Judea (19:3–9) is a direct confrontation with the Pharisees in which they are said to "test him" (as in 16:1). Their question concerns the legal reason for permitting divorce "for any cause?" The narrative background for such a question is clear; Jesus just spoke to the disciples about forgiveness and patience in the face of difficulty. So the Pharisees, whose "territory" Jesus has entered, put a traditionally difficult question before him. He answers by referring to the OT account of creation. However, he uses the antagonistic introduction "have you not read?" implying that they have indeed read but not understood the message. The Pharisees have a good point, however, in that Jesus' answer contradicts Deut. 24:1–4. Jesus replies by acknowledging the conflict but asserting that its cause is not

God but humanity's hardness of heart. An exception is allowed (un-chastity) but it is not God's primary intention. Jesus concludes with a phrase that emphasizes his authority ("I say to you") and places the exception in a legalistic form. Thus the original question is answered in the affirmative only in the sense that there is *one* and only one reason for divorce; Jesus affirms what had been said earlier about the reasons for divorce (5:31). The Pharisees, then, appear to be obstructive and threatening while Jesus is presented affirming the will and intention of the Father.

DISCIPLES ADMONISHED AND ADVISED (19:23—20:34)

The disciples then comment (19:10–12) that if such is the case, it is better not to marry. Their reason for arriving at this conclusion is not clear and the reader must fill in the gap. Jesus' reply supplies the context, that is, he comments that the reception of this precept is a gift. The disciples, therefore, were complaining that if there is a chance of trouble or difficulty, it is not worth getting involved; that is, take the safe way out. But Jesus continues, telling them that suffering and persecution are part of this road and that although the Father will help, he will not remove all obstacles. The narrator, in reporting the incident, has given us further insight into the disciples' lack of comprehension and, of course, a corroboration of the teaching on divorce. The deeper implications of the saying about eunuchs is underlined with the final statement of admonition.

With an indefinite "then" (19:13–15), the narrator reports that children were brought to him so that he could bless them; family imagery continues. It was at the beginning of chap. 18 when Jesus admonished the disciples to be like humble children. Here in chap. 19, the disciples rebuke the people who bring their children but Jesus interrupts with a statement that is reminiscent of a beatitude. The narrator tells us that Jesus does as the parents request and then departs, perhaps indicating an end to a phase of his teaching.

In these first fifteen verses of chap. 19, Jesus entered the territory of the Pharisees (and his enemies in general) and, after rebuking them, rebuffed his disciples twice. In each instance, the topic is related to family matters and illustrates the high demands that are placed on his followers, even though they may not be able to comply. The emphasis on receiving a gift from God (19:11) echoes the positive response of Peter in 16:21 when Jesus told him that his insight and confession came from the Father.

The narrator leaves us guessing about the protagonist in the next incident (19:16–22), calling him "one." Since Jesus was speaking to the disciples in the preceding paragraph, the reader will probably assume that it is one of the disciples, especially since he addresses Jesus as "Teacher." His question, however, is naive, even for the disciples, since it implies that "a good (deed)" will gain eternal life. The result is that the question appears to be another testing of Jesus. He responds first with a question about the reason for asking him about what is good. "One there is who is good." Jesus himself acts with humility, just as he requires it of his followers, and, in the process, acknowledges his own source of authority.

He tells the questioner: Keep the commandments. When asked, "Which?" he replies with a list of commandments: don't kill, don't commit adultery, don't steal, don't witness falsely, honor your parents, and love your neighbor as yourself. Jesus' understanding of the commandments was clearly stated in the Sermon on the Mount (5:21–44), where they were radicalized, and the final commandment in this list ("Love your neighbor as yourself") was the final item in the antitheses (5:43–44). The questioner, identified as a young man, claims to have "observed all these" and asks what he still lacks. There is no indication why he should ask such a question and the reader must speculate about what he expects; somehow he knows this isn't enough. This attitude will affect the reader, leading him to take a more positive view of the young man. Jesus' response indicates what the narrator has in mind: "If you would be perfect . . . sell what you have and . . . follow me" (19:21). The word "perfect" was important in the Sermon on the Mount (5:48), where it was used to summarize the demands of Jesus and the character of the Father. Jesus requires a full commitment to the way of the kingdom. But when in the last sentence the young man is also described as "rich," his unwillingness to make such a complete change is clearer. He went away full of sorrow, we are told.

Thus what had appeared at first to be another test and perhaps another attack from the Pharisees is instead a portrait of a follower who is unable to accept Jesus' hard demands. His attachment to possessions is too great. Nevertheless, his "sorrow" indicates that his interest in eternal life was sincere.

Following this confrontation with the rich young follower, Jesus speaks to his disciples (19:23–30). By reporting these general statements here, the narrator explains the lesson of the confrontation. The issue is still entry into the kingdom of heaven. The analogy in 19:24 of the camel and the eye of the needle underlines the accuracy of the previous incident. The "astonished" disciples ask, then, how anyone could enter. The narrator tells us that Jesus "looked at them" before speaking, implying that he wonders why they ask such a question. The answer is consistent with the earlier saying about eunuchs: God can do the impossible. When Peter says, in effect, that *we* are not rich, what shall we have? the reader is again reminded of the negative character of the disciples. The saying emphasizes that future rewards are not material and that they require extreme singleness of purpose, expressed in terms of leaving to follow Jesus. The final generalized saying about the reversal of first and last sums up the demands. The reference to the twelve thrones has, of course, implications about the superiority of Jesus' way over that of traditional Judaism. The rewards are eschatological; the Son of man is one who judges.

Some further implications about these rewards and demands are illustrated immediately by the parable of the vineyard (20:1–16). The story tells about the grace of God and his willingness to do what is "unfair." The ending (20:16) is the same as the ending of the twelve thrones saying, that is, the first will be last. The Twelve should now be able to understand parables (as in chap. 13) and they apparently do; there is no comment to the contrary. The key phrase is: "Whatever is right I will give to you." The narrator tells the story from the householder's point of view. The final words to the grumbling workers read literally: "Is your eye evil because I am good?" (usually translated: "Do you begrudge my generosity?"). The phrase "evil eye" appeared in a short parable in the Sermon on the Mount (6:22–3): an evil or unsound eye results in a body full of darkness. Here in Matthew 20, it obviously refers to the grumblers' response to the householder's goodness. Even though they receive fair wages, they spitefully condemn the goodness of the householder. By adding the statement about the eschatological reversal (last first, first last), the reader is reminded of the preceding emphasis on riches and rewards. The promise of the future life should outweigh the inequities and difficulties of the present.

The narrator notes a change of location, from Judea to the ascent to Jerusalem, during which journey Jesus tells his disciples, for the third time, that the Son of man will be condemned, crucified, and then rise. The reader has, of course, heard this before but it is now explicitly restated as Jesus nears the city. The disciples' reaction is not recorded but the next incident illustrates for the reader their low level of comprehension. The mother of James and John, two of the first

followers, requests that her sons have a privileged place in the kingdom. When Jesus asks them if they can "drink the cup that I drink,"
they reply that they can. The meaning of the symbol "cup" is obvious
to the reader since Jesus has just predicted his passion and death.
Given the track record of the disciples, the reader will have to decide
whether they really do understand. Jesus' reply indicates that he
takes them seriously but, as is his practice, he acknowledges the
source of his authority and the subordinate position that he and they
occupy. The Father will give it to those "for whom it has been
prepared."

The other ten disciples are indignant, apparently because they
think that someone has been given an advantage over them. This
leads Jesus to state again, in a different way, the "first-last" principle.
The great person is a servant. The most important example is, of
course, the fact that the Son of man came to serve and to give his life
as a ransom for many. This is a crucial statement: Jesus himself,
whose authority is supreme, explains the significance of his death as a
ransom. It is the only time the word "ransom" appears in the story
and the reader is likely to connect it with the explanation of Jesus'
name: "He will save his people from their sins." The Son of man has
been described both as a judge and also as one who suffers.

Another geographic notice signals a new section of the story. Two
blind men call Jesus "Son of David" and ask for mercy. This is very
similar to a previous story in 9:27–31. In this instance, the crowd
rebukes the two blind men but Jesus heals them and they follow him.
The reader, of course, already knows the accuracy of the title Son of
David since the narrator used it in the opening sentence (1:1) and in
three other places in connection with healings (9:27; 12:23; 15:22).
The narrative emphasis is on the men's persistence and confidence in
Jesus. When Jesus heals them, the narrator reports that he felt pity
(compassion) toward them, a comment that the narrator has used
before to describe Jesus' attitude.

INITIAL STATEMENT IN THE TEMPLE (21:1–22)

The geographical note at 21:1 indicates further progress on the road
from Jericho (20:29) to Jerusalem. The disciples are sent out to find
the ass and her colt. If questioned, they need merely say that "the
Lord has need of them." Jesus is presented by the narrator as knowing that this answer will satisfy whoever objects. His foreknowledge
is directly connected with God's plan in the fulfillment quotation that

follows. The quote, from Zech. 9:9, refers to the coming of the king. This is the first time that Jesus is called or implied to be king. Although he has been preaching about the kingdom of heaven, the title "king" has not been used. It anticipates a more frequent use in the rest of the story, albeit with varied intentions.

The narrator tells us that after the disciples follow his instructions, Jesus sits on the two animals ("them") and the crowd responds by spreading garments and branches on the road in front of him. They acclaim him "Son of David" (again) and the one who comes in the Lord's name. The crowd, in effect, interprets the significance of the event for the reader. The crowd has often been presented favorably, but not necessarily as reliable. In this instance, the repeated use of the Son of David, in conjunction with the verification of the fulfillment quotation, and with Jesus' own command to the disciples, combine to create a positive image of the acclamation of the crowd.

The "procession" apparently takes place on the Mount of Olives, for the narrator says in 21:10, "when he entered the city." The question about his identity is answered by the "crowds": "This is the prophet Jesus of Nazareth from Galilee" (21:11). The reader will wonder why this identification is different from the acclamation. It is not clear, at first, what the narrator is implying; the reader focuses attention on the identification of Jesus. The next event (21:12–13), however, helps to clarify the narrator's point of view because when Jesus enters the temple he acts and speaks as a prophet. He ejects merchants, disrupts the money-changers and quotes Jeremiah: "My house shall be called a house of prayer." It is interesting that Jesus himself is quoted as using the "it is written" introduction to the quotation. Typically, the narrator also mentions that the blind and lame came to him "in the temple" where he healed them. The reaction of the people would reemphasize the prophetic character of his activity. Then, when the narrator subsequently reports the reactions of the chief priests and scribes, the connection to the third passion prediction is obvious. Specifically, the narrator says that when they saw the "remarkable" things Jesus did *and that the children were calling him Son of David,* they were indignant. The mention of children prepares the reader for the quote that follows because when the Pharisees ask if he heard what the children are saying, Jesus answers antagonistically by asking, "Have you never read?" and then quotes Ps. 8:2. We are not told how the authorities respond; the impression we are left with is that they retreat in defeat. Nevertheless, Jesus leaves the temple and stays overnight in Bethany.

On the way back to the temple the next morning (21:18), the narrator says that Jesus is hungry and curses a fig tree because it bears no fruit. It withered at once! The disciples ask, Why? Jesus answers that they too could do such things if they had "faith and never doubt"; it is what they ask for in prayer, with faith, that they will receive. But the reader knows that they fall far short of such an ideal.

DISAGREEMENT ABOUT AUTHORITY (21:23-46)

The following incident (21:23-27) reveals the narrator's point. When Jesus reenters the temple, the authorities ask what his authority is to do such things! The reader will think of the fig tree as well as the cleansing and healing, even though the questioners know nothing about them; that is, the authorities will be perceived as truly inept. Jesus' authority comes from the Father, as the reference to prayer makes clear, so the supposedly religious people fail to see the hand of God in the action of Jesus.

Since the opponents clearly lack faith, Jesus' reply is an attempt to show that they purposely ignore the obvious. The narrator relies on a seldom used technique—a report of their own inner discussion. Notice that they do not worry about what is actually true but rather about what effect each answer will have on the audience or on their authority. Thus the narrator portrays them seeking a winning (or face-saving) argument, not as seekers of truth. They take the easy way out and answer that they do not know the source of John the Baptist's authority. The narrator has made sure that we recognize this cowardly response. And since they have demonstrated their lack of willingness to commit themselves, Jesus is quoted as saying that he, in turn, will not answer *their* question (21:27). The duplicity of the opponents is clearly portrayed.

But the narrator continues the report of Jesus' reply, another rhetorical question (What do you think?) followed by the parable of the two sons (21:28-32). The incident is unusual in that Jesus, after the story, asks the chief priests and elders to name the obedient son, an answer obvious from the story. Then Jesus draws his conclusion: tax collectors and harlots go into the kingdom before "you" because they believed John the Baptist. Now the connection between the parable and the question about authority is clear. The religious authorities do not want to acknowledge Jesus' authority even though it is displayed before them. The repetition of "repent" in the parable (about the obedient son's change of mind), and in the final sentence ("you did not afterward repent"), underlines the key issue. Jesus' first statement (and John the Baptist's, too) was "Repent and believe in the gospel" (4:17; cf. 3:2); the authorities will not acknowledge the origin of either John or Jesus. The other key phrase in the incident is "the way of righteousness," which Jesus uses to describe John the Baptist's mission. In chap. 11 Jesus had praised John as a true prophet and yet as the least in the kingdom of heaven. Here, there is no question at all about his authority.

The next parable is narrated without a pause (21:33–42). It is the familiar story of the owner of a vineyard (a householder) whose share of the fruit is kept by the tenants. After the tenants beat, kill, and stone the servants he sends to collect the rent, the tenants kill the owner's son because, they say, he is the heir. The chief priests and elders respond in the obvious way when Jesus asks them what they expect the owner to do: kill the tenants and replace them with responsible people. The reader expects Jesus to draw out the implications of the story, attacking the chief priests and elders. But he first quotes Ps. 118:22–23 which speaks about a stone that, though rejected by the builders, becomes the "head of the corner" because the Lord chooses it. "Therefore, the kingdom of God will be taken away from you and given to a nation producing the fruits of it" (21:43). Although this conclusion is not as direct as the previous summary (21:32), the reader will, of course, see the connection between the authorities and the tenants who are removed from the vineyard. The analogy about producing fruits is not only directly relevant to the parable but is also connected with the incident associated with the temple, the cursing of the fig tree; it was cursed because it had produced no fruit. The image of fruit was also prominent in John the Baptist's message (3:8, 10), in the sermon (7:16–20), in the response to the Beelzebul accusation (12:33), and twice in parables in chap. 13 (13:8, 26). In most of these cases, the context is controversy.

To make sure that the reader has understood the full implication of the stories, the narrator reports that the "chief priests and Pharisees" realized that Jesus was speaking about them (21:45). Notice that the narrator explicitly mentions the Pharisees, who were not mentioned in the earlier portions of the chapter. Finally, because they understand, they try to arrest him but refrain because the crowd considers Jesus to be a prophet.

Thus, the contrast is carefully defined. Jesus' entry into Jerusalem was described in "triumphant" imagery, making special use of the Son of David and his place in God's plan. Jesus' prophetic activity in the temple led to direct confrontation and the attack on his authority by those who claim to be true leaders of the religious establishment. The narrator placed the material in a significant order, especially the striking event of the fig tree, to encourage the reader to make the proper connections. It is only at the end of each incident that an interpretation occurs, if then. The final note about the crowds will gently remind the reader about the triumphal entry and also reinforce the contrast between the crowds and the local religious authorities.

THE CONTROVERSY INTENSIFIES (22:1–46)

The next section begins with a narrator's note: Jesus continues to speak in parables. Since the parables told in this part of the narrative have been used primarily to criticize the opponents, and are not like the kingdom parables of Matthew 13, the reader will anticipate that the controversy will continue, and he will not be disappointed. After the story of the killing of the servants in the vineyard, the fact that the king's servants are killed in the next parable (22:1–14), about a marriage feast will be somewhat less shocking. The king's repeated efforts and his total lack of success make him similar to the owner of the vineyard. Nevertheless, the destruction of "their" city does seem excessive. This kind of extreme action forces the reader to look for the symbols it implies. The feast is eventually attended by guests who come from "the streets." The story concludes with the king casting out a guest who does not have a wedding garment. Since this incident seems out of place, it adds to the reader's involvement, forcing some kind of explanatory hypothesis.

The conclusion to the parable (22:11–14) not only raises a difficult problem of interpretation, but it is stated in words that repeat a theme stressed earlier; the eschatological phrase ("cast him into outer darkness") was employed in 8:12 to describe the sons of the kingdom who do not measure up to the standard the centurion represents. "Weeping and gnashing of teeth" occurs six times in Matthew's story (8:12; 13:42, 50; 22:13; 24:51; 25:30) and dramatizes the reality of God's punishment. The final statement, distinguishing between calling and choosing, is likely to cause the reader trouble. The parable itself only mentions one person being cast out. Even though the phrase "being chosen" has not been mentioned before, the idea that God can intervene in these affairs is common enough, especially in incidents such as Peter's confession. The chosen people are those who were not invited initially but who have an opportunity to join the feast after the first group refuses. Since the story is clearly addressed to the opponents, the affront to the Pharisees need not be stated.

The narrator, however, makes it perfectly clear how enraged they are; we are told that they conspire to entangle Jesus, apparently hoping he will condemn himself. The deviousness of this move is stressed when the narrator says they sent their disciples, with the Herodians, not only to ask a question, but to compliment him, hoping to catch him off guard. The question itself is a classic one for Judaism, the conflict between king and Lord. In another rare intrusion from the narrator, Jesus is said to "be aware of their malice." Then he reportedly attacks them directly, letting them know that he is aware of their motives. "Why put me to the test, you hypocrites?" (22:18). The narrator has already told us that the Pharisees have tried to test him, and thus Jesus is presented as perceptive and full of insight. The word hypocrite has been used before, but it was not until 15:7 that it was directly associated with the Pharisees. It is appropriate in the current context because of the false compliment paid to Jesus in the preceding verses. But since Jesus is not taken in, the earlier implied evaluation of the Pharisees is confirmed. Jesus' response is cagey; he does not walk into their trap. The narrator tells us they "marveled" and had to retreat saying nothing.

"The same day" another faction, the Sadducees, come to question Jesus (22:23). The reader, of course, already expects an attitude similar to the Pharisees'. We are told that the Sadducees do not believe in a resurrection (22:23); nevertheless, they ask a question based on the concept of a resurrection. The situation they describe is bizarre but not impossible. Jesus responds that they are wrong, knowing neither Scripture nor God's power; first, marriage is a human institution and thus not a factor in heaven. In the second place, since he knows that they do not accept the idea of a resurrection, Jesus proceeds to argue from the only text that the Sadducees will accept, the Torah, that there is indeed a witness to the resurrection in the books of Moses! Typically, the narrator does not tell us what the Sadducees do or say; the reader gets the impression that they retreat saying nothing. The crowd, however, is described as astonished "at his teaching." Thus by combining these attacks and then subsequently reporting Jesus' victory over his opponents, the basis for their determination to get rid of him is explained.

The attack continues when the Pharisees hear about how Jesus bested the Sadducees (22:34) and, we can assume, want to try once again to show up both Jesus and the Sadducees. This time a "lawyer" asks about the "greatest commandment." The narrator tells us, once more, that his purpose was to test Jesus. Jesus responds by quoting both Deut. 6:5 and Lev. 19:18 about love of God and neighbor. The absence of response gives the reader the impression that the lawyer is speechless and that his attempt to test Jesus did not work out as he expected. The concluding statement (22:40) focuses on the law and prophets, first mentioned at the beginning of the Sermon on the Mount (in 5:17) when Jesus says he came to fulfill the law and prophets, not abolish them. Later in that sermon, the Golden Rule (7:12) was equated with "the law and the prophets." Now the message of love is characterized the same way.

The narrator now informs us that Jesus asks the Pharisees a question: "Whose son is the Christ?" Their answer, the Son of David, is rejected by Jesus because David would not call his own son "Lord" (22:45). In effect, Jesus demonstrates his own knowledge of the Scriptures and his ability to argue with the so-called scholars. The narrator concludes this incident, and the whole section of controversies, with a summary statement (22:46) that reaffirms Jesus' status by telling the reader not only that he had defeated them but that no one *dared* to ask him another question, implying that they not only admit defeat, but that they were silenced.

THE INDICTMENT OF THE OPPONENTS (23:1–39)

The next paragraph opens with another vague comment about the audience, but there is no indication of any change of place or time. The crowds and disciples are mentioned, but not the Pharisees. Jesus begins to speak by describing the "scribes and Pharisees"; notice the absence of the Sadducees. And although the audience has changed somewhat, the tone and topic have not. As noted earlier, a long speech can affect the reader by confirming, changing, or modifying his image of the speaker and his reliability. In this opening statement (23:1–3), Jesus' remarks are directed to the crowds and disciples who are encouraged to follow the *advice* of the scribes and Pharisees but not their practice. The point he makes is reminiscent of the Sermon on the Mount (5:20). Jesus had told his followers that their righteousness must exceed that of the scribes and Pharisees. In 6:1–18, although the scribes and Pharisees are not mentioned, Jesus describes hypocrites who act in order to be seen by their peers. The coordination of advice and deed has been a major issue right from the beginning; John the

Baptist mentioned it and the importance of good fruits has been maintained throughout the narration by the narrator. After describing the conceit of the scribes and Pharisees, Jesus advises his listeners not to expect special honorific titles. "Call no man Rabbi" or "father" because you have "one Father who is in heaven . . ." and one master, the Christ. The theme of humility and service is stressed with words that are reminiscent of 20:20, just prior to the entry into the city. And the issue of humbleness, similiar to that in 18:4, is also stated in the language of reversal, a technique used often by the narrator.

The next paragraph (23:13–15) presents a problem. It appears at first to be addressed to the scribes and Pharisees. But the reader has been led to think of them as recalcitrant and independent, set in their ways and unwilling to recognize Jesus' authority. Thus it becomes clear that this woe is not directed toward the scribes and Pharisees but is a rhetorical device intended to instruct the followers by describing the opponents, the antitype of the disciple. As a result, the first woe describes the nondisciple as closing the door to the kingdom of heaven, the opposite of Jesus' task and mission. The second woe (23:15), equally terse, attacks the scribes and Pharisees for misusing their zeal and devotion.

It is clear to the reader now that repetition is a technique of this part of the story. The term "hypocrite," continuing the comment in 22:18, is clarified by example.

The Pharisees are called blind guides (see the indictment of them earlier in 15:14). The issue here is taking an oath, something Jesus said in the Sermon on the Mount was unnecessary. The alleged argument of the Pharisees makes distinctions between either the temple and its gold or the altar and the gift placed upon it. The style is also reminiscent of the antitheses of the Sermon on the Mount. The rebuff, however, is not "but I say to you," rather it is a rhetorical question, implying that the distinction is perverse. The paragraph ends with a statement bringing the topic back to the one that is always central to Jesus, the authority of the Father over all his creatures (23:22).

The fourth woe also mentions "hypocrites" who neglect the primary demands of the law while concentrating on the minutiae which are *not* required. When "blind guides" is repeated in 23:24, it is clear that the reader should consider these terms to be equivalent.

Matthew's use of parabolic language continues with an accusation that the "cup" and "plate" are full of extortion and rapacity (23:25).

Since these terms are unique in the narrative, the reader must supply the intended extension. It is most likely the scribes and Pharisees that he is describing.

Such an inference is confirmed in the next precise comparison: you are like "tombs." The phrase "full of hypocrisy and iniquity" parallels "extortion and rapacity." Verse 28 then returns to the initial point—the scribes and Pharisees appear righteous but they are not.

The final woe (23:29–36) is a lengthy indictment that again penetrates the facade that the scribes and Pharisees have erected. Claiming to be righteous, they illustrate, when they reject Jesus, how much they resemble their earthly "fathers" rather than the "Father in heaven." The description of the treatment of the prophets helps confirm the interpretation of the parable of the vineyard when the Son and servants are murdered. Also, "brood of vipers" recalls the critical preaching of John the Baptist; the implication is that they were involved in the arrest or persecution of John—something that is never made explicit in the narrative. The seriousness of these accusations is emphasized with a prediction about punishment in Gehenna. Jesus says he "is sending prophets, wise men and scribes" who will be persecuted and killed. The combined effect on the reader will be to equate the disciples, previously described, with the prophets. This theme was especially prominent in Matthew 10 when Jesus described the fate that awaits his followers. The apocalyptic overtones were present there also. The Pharisees will be responsible for all the "righteous blood" shed on the earth.

Therefore, Matthew 23, a series of woes prefaced by a description of the opponents, describes the duplicity of the hypocrites and concludes with a prediction of their ultimate rejection.

The next paragraph (23:37–39) requires the reader to readjust because Jesus addresses Jerusalem rather than the scribes and Pharisees. The connection between his opponents and Jerusalem was already noted in chaps. 15 and 19. The city represents the Pharisees; both are accused of killing the prophets. But now Jesus speaks in the first person, reminding the reader of those earlier moments, such as 11:25–30, when his intimacy with the Father was clearly stated. Here he speaks as Wisdom (already hinted at in 23:34). The son, and his Father, want to protect their children, but their help is not acceptable. As a result, the fate of the city is sealed. You will not see me, he says, until you act as my followers did in chap. 21 when I approached the city: "Blessed is he who comes in the name of the Lord."

THE IMPORTANCE OF RESPONDING
TO JESUS (24:1—25:46)

Matthew 24 opens with a geographical notice: "Jesus left the temple and was going away." This takes him outside the city to the place from which he entered, the Mount of Olives, overlooking the temple. The narrator tells us that the disciples "point out to him" the buildings of the temple; for what purpose we are not told. Jesus' answer, however, continues the emphasis on the future begun at the end of the previous section. Using the emphatic introduction, "Truly, I say to you," he predicts that there will be a time when the walls and buildings of the temple will be thrown down. The connection with the previous lament over the city (23:37–38) is obvious; the "house" of Jerusalem will be desolate. The disciples do not understand the saying because they ask, again, about the timing of these events. Notice, however, that it is now a question about Jesus' connection to the end, a fact they assume. The phrase "the sign of your coming" is new, although the coming of the Son of man has been mentioned often enough. But it is interesting that the narrator encourages us to equate the "sign of your coming" with "the close of the age." The question, then, indicates the extent of their progress or learning.

After this introduction, the narrator relates a long connected speech (24:4—25:46). It begins with a warning about the "many" who will claim to be the Messiah and will lead many people astray. There will be other apparent "signs" of the end, but they are not *the* signs. International conflict, famine, and earthquake will merely mark the beginning of the suffering.

The sufferings are described: tribulation, death, hatred; betrayal will be common; false prophets will be active. But the "gospel of the kingdom" will be preached everywhere: "Then the end will come" (24:14).

The reader is reminded of the troubles that Jesus has already predicted, especially in chap. 10 in connection with the missionary activity of his followers. Since that part of the story, we have been shown the growing enmity of the opponents; *now* the Father will wait no longer.

In Matt. 24:15 the details of the close of this age are narrated. Because Jesus' reliability has been firmly established, he, rather than the narrator, describes the future.

The desolating sacrilege (24:15) standing in the holy place is not defined but the "aside" in the same verse ("Let the reader understand") is an overt hint to the reader that it is a parabolic saying which, presumably, the disciples can interpret correctly. When the abomination appears, flee! This final tribulation surpasses all other troubles, even though the Father has shortened them because of the elect. The coming of the Son of man will be sudden and obvious, so do not be misled. The cryptic saying in 24:28 about eagles or vultures implies destruction or decay and death.

After this tribulation is described, Jesus states that there will be cosmic signs (24:29–31), including the sign of the Son of man which appears to be defined in the following sentences, that is, he is coming with angels to call the elect.

Having voiced these warnings, describing the situation to come, the remainder of the speech is composed primarily of admonitions that stress the importance of heeding this advice. Since the disciples have already been trained to see the deeper significance of parabolic speech, the rest of the speech, composed primarily of parabolic sayings and full-fledged parables, should be clear. The first saying states that the budding of a fig tree is an indication that the end is near. The reader cannot miss the point; interpretation is encouraged at the outset—"learn its parable (lesson)"—and the following sentence makes the lesson specific (24:33). The proximity of the end is emphasized in the following verse ("this generation," 24:34). The connection between vv. 34 and 35 is not clear. The reader will have to adjust to the two meanings of "pass away."

Although he is thoroughly reliable, even Jesus does not know the Father's schedule. The connection between this statement and the previous statement is clear when we realize that the comment about Noah describes the destruction of a people who failed to prepare for the future. "Son of man" continues to be used in connection with judgmental images, and the suddenness of his return continues to be expressed in images of work, in the field or at a mill. Matt. 24:42, which contains the word "watch," anticipates the next parable. Thus the reader is carefully guided by the sequence of admonition, parable, and admonition; you know that he will come, but since you do not know the time, be constantly prepared.

In Matt. 24:25 another parable is then told, this time starting with a question that helps the reader see the point, that is, the difference between a faithful, wise servant and a foolish servant. The concluding beatitude underlines the point. Notice that although the arrangement of the material is a bit unusual, the conclusion helps orient the reader to the wider purpose that the narrator has, that is, the repetition of the word "hypocrites," the first occurrence in chap. 24. It helps to bind the condemnation stated so emphatically in chap. 23 to "this generation" and the symbolic language of chap. 24. The conclusion ("weeping and gnashing of teeth") contains a theme found earlier in 8:12, 13:42, 50, and 22:13.

The next paragraph (25:1–13) begins with a more traditional opening for a parable, one that focuses on the kingdom of heaven. The description of the virgins as wise and foolish follows smoothly from the opening of the previous paragraph (24:45) about the wise and foolish servants. Their wisdom is demonstrated in their preparation, taking along a supply of oil. As the story explains, the wise virgins are thus able to meet the bridegroom (later called the Lord) because they are prepared to wait; they have planned ahead. The foolish, left outside, are finally rejected by the Lord. The admonition ("Watch") from 24:42 is repeated at the conclusion.

The image of the bridegroom is not new; in 9:15, when the opposition to Jesus was beginning to increase, Jesus refers to himself as the bridegroom who, because he is now present, should elicit celebration, not fasting. Now, in 25:1–13, the marriage feast is closed to those who are not properly prepared. They are left in the dark.

The next parable (25:14–30) begins with a very vague opening which forces the reader to make some connection with the opening of the previous parable, that is, "for it will be" when the kingdom of God comes. This is a longer, more elaborate parable about large sums of money and the varied response of those who receive them. The parable moves quickly to the return of the "master" and his accounting of each servant's action. The first two are congratulated fully. The third servant's rationale is turned against him: "You knew that. . . ." The master himself condemns the servant and throws him out into outer darkness where men weep and gnash their teeth. The reader's attention is directed back to the "parable chapter" where the same phrase was used, there in connection with the interpretation of the parables! The disciples were told in Matthew 13 that they had been given the secrets of the kingdom. Thus we have two clues about what the parable means: (1) the parallel between talents and secrets, and (2) the eschatological punishment that results from a neglect of gifts. Whatever the gift, it must be used; the fig tree (or good tree) should produce fruit.

This long speech ends with another parable (25:31–46) that begins with the words "when the Son of man returns." The issue now is not "whether" or "when" it will be but "what" it will be like. The introduction is full of eschatological imagery: angels, throne, and the gathering of all nations. But in 25:34 the judge is called "king" and those blessed (cf. the Beatitudes: 5:3–11) are invited to inherit the kingdom because they have cared for the king. The narrator calls the "blessed ones" the "righteous" and reports that they are puzzled about the king's statement. The answer is simple: "as you did it to the least of these my brethren. . . ." Those who do not act this way are cursed. The narrator ends by commenting that they are punished eternally, while the righteous live eternally. Matt. 26:1 marks the formal ending of this last major speech of Jesus.

The parabolic content of Jesus' final speech to his disciples is significant. There is no indication, as yet, that they did not understand it and the reader is encouraged to assume that they have. Also, it repeats the theme of righteousness that was first stated at the very beginning of Jesus' ministry and exemplified by Joseph's obedience (1:18—2:23). In addition, the speech reemphasizes the need for mutual love, the care that another may require, as a proper fulfillment of the great commandment. Finally, it also stresses another major element in the story, the gift-giving of the Father as the source of righteousness (especially in the final parable).

6

The Conflict Takes Place

26:1—28:20

After the long speech in the previous chapters (Matthew 23—25), the narrative resumes in chap. 26. The narrator reminds the reader of the previous predictions about suffering and death. For the first time, however, the Passover is mentioned in connection with the suffering. In addition to establishing a date, we are also alerted to the fact that events are moving to a climax.

Having set the context, the narrator reports a meeting of the chief priests and elders to plan Jesus' arrest, quoting them as saying that they realize that any action against Jesus should be postponed until after the feast because of a possible unfriendly reaction from the people. Thus the stage is set: Jesus' often predicted suffering is now being actively planned by his opponents.

THE PASSOVER CELEBRATION IN JERUSALEM (26:6-29)

Matt. 26:6 contains another vague time designation and also a change of place; while staying in a suburban home, Jesus is anointed with expensive oil. The disciples misunderstand once again: they are indignant at the waste. They fail to see its significance in the light of Jesus' impending death, that is, they do not see it as a preburial anointing. It is apparently this incident that triggers Judas' decision, reported in the next verses, to go to the authorities to betray Jesus to them. The narrator does not report what Judas' motive is, but implies (with a question) that he is interested in the money. We are encouraged, then, to think of Judas as a disciple worried about the "waste," as described in the previous incident

The disciples initiate the celebration of Passover by asking where they should prepare for the meal (26:17). Jesus explains and they follow his orders. Since he is open with his plans, he is obviously not hiding from Judas.

The supper is clearly a Passover meal which Jesus celebrates with the Twelve. But since Passover has been associated with death, when he says that one of the Twelve will betray him it comes as no surprise to the reader. But the reaction of the disciples seems rather mild: "They were very sorrowful" (26:21). Then, when each disciple asks, in turn, "Is it I, Lord?" (26:22), the reader must account for their uncertainty. The most obvious way to fill in this gap is to assume that they fail to see the seriousness of the betrayal. If they are really unsure about whether they have betrayed Jesus, it may be because they think it is something either far removed from the present or trivial.

Jesus' answer is vague: it is one of you. And, he warns, it is a serious decision (26:23–24). When Judas, called the betrayer by the narrator and already known to the reader as the betrayer, asks Jesus if *he* is the one, the narrator has effectively portrayed his duplicity. Jesus' answer ("You have said so") is very revealing to the reader, even though its implications might be missed by the disciples.

Matt. 26:26 begins the account of the distribution and eating of the bread and wine. The narrator does not tell us anything about the disciples' response; we must assume that they understand its significance even though they have often misunderstood in similar situations. The narrator places the reader in an ambivalent position.

The language Jesus employs is familiar in most instances, especially the reference in 26:28 to the blood that is "poured out for many for the forgiveness of sins." Jesus' very name means he will "save them from sins" (see 1:21) even though the word "covenant" appears only here in Matthew. Blood is mentioned in connection with the prophets in 23:30–35, with Judas in 27:4–8, and with Pilate and the people in 27:24–25. The reference to "not drinking again" helps to establish the point that the decisive event is imminent; Jesus anticipates the arrival of the father's kingdom.

THE SON'S OBEDIENCE AND THE
DISCIPLES' FAILURE (26:30–56)

The transition to the Mount of Olives seems abrupt. Jesus makes another prediction that we assume will come true and it is made even more effective because he himself (not the narrator) quotes Zech. 13:7, about sheep being scattered when the shepherd is struck. By telling the disciples that they will "fall away," he indicates that they are really betrayers. There is a positive side, however; after he is raised, "I will go before you into Galilee" (26:30), an indirect way of telling the reader that they will not go so far as to become his opponents.

Peter, once again, declares his good intentions and Jesus, again, predicts his failure. Just as he represented Satan previously, so also here.

The next paragraph (26:36–46) begins with another change of location, a "place called Gethsemane." Although the narrator tells us that Jesus was sorrowful (notice again the omniscient point of view), Jesus himself is quoted as saying he is sorrowful in the next verse. The three disciples—Peter, James, and John—who witnessed the transfiguration (17:1–8) are selected once again. But when Jesus returns after praying, their failure to endure is forcefully portrayed—three times.

Jesus' prayer, which the narrator quotes even though Jesus is said to be alone, focuses on the obedience of the Son; he accepts whatever the Father requires. This not only shows his attitude to the Father, but also restates the theme of God's control over events. The threefold repetition of the request and acquiescence will affect the reader by highlighting the contrast between Jesus' stability/obedience and the weakness of the disciples. Verse 41 repeats (1) the admonition from chaps. 24 and 25 about watching and (2) the contrast between the flesh and spirit, here stated in proverbial form. "Flesh" has not been used this way before; it was used previously to refer to human beings.

When Jesus returns the third time, he adds, "Behold, the hour is at hand, and the Son of man is betrayed into the hands of sinners" (26:45). The verb "is at hand" has been used previously for (1) the coming of the kingdom of heaven (3:2; 4:17; 10:7), (2) the time of harvest (21:34), and (3) Jesus' arrival in Jerusalem (21:1). Here in 26:45–46 it appears twice in close succession, describing both "the hour" and the betrayer. Does this mean the kingdom has arrived? It could. The word "hour" is used in a similar way at 24:44: "Therefore you also must be ready; for the Son of man is coming at an hour you do not expect." (See also 24:50; 25:13). Here in Gethsemane, although the disciples are told to watch, they "take their rest," which means the hour has come at a time they did not expect, just as Jesus had warned. The betrayal is the work of an insider who cooperates with the religious authorities. One of the Twelve, the followers, has brought the confrontation to a head. This signals, in a special way, the importance of the following events. The reader is being guided to prepare for the final conflict and its ultimate implications.

The betrayer completes his treachery with an ironic act of friendship (26:47–50). The narrator makes certain that we notice the irony by quoting Judas's comment to the authorities; we must suppose that it took place sometime earlier in the evening. Judas is indeed a betrayer with no remorse. Jesus' response is ambiguous and thus hard to translate; it could be sarcastic ("Why are you here?") or direct ("Do what you have come to do") or challenging ("What kind of deal did you make?").

Since the authorities have come armed, it is not surprising that one of Jesus' companions (unnamed and not called a disciple) cuts off the ear of a slave of the high priest (26:51). This violent reaction to the seizure of Jesus sets the stage for the rest of the story. Violence is not necessary, Jesus says, because the Father would intervene if it was appropriate, a reminder of the theme of the Gethsemane prayers. The Scriptures are fulfilled because Jesus is obedient to the Father's will, as we have heard so often, beginning with the baptism. To emphasize the point, the narrator says in 26:55 that Jesus spoke to the crowd "at that hour," another phrase from the Gethsemane incident. The Scripture is fulfilled, he says, because they came to seize him at night away from the crowds, even though they had plenty of opportunity during the day in the temple. The incident ends with the narrator reporting that "all the disciples forsook him and fled."

THE PERSECUTION AND TRIALS (26:57—27:66)

Jesus' trial before the high priest and the council is interwoven with the denial of Peter. As Jesus is led away, the narrator tells us that Peter followed at a distance, that is, he did not completely desert Jesus. But we are not told its significance until after the main events of the inquest are narrated, thus holding the reader's attention. The narrator's report begins by informing us that although the authorities sought "false witnesses," the evidence was not admissible. So the high priest is forced to ask Jesus to comment on the accusation about destroying and rebuilding the temple. The reader is aware, of course, that this is not something Jesus is reported to have said in the story. Jesus is silent (26:63). When asked directly if he is Christ and Son of God, Jesus replies in the affirmative. Notice how this incident parallels the confession of Peter in 14:22–23 and 16:13–20 and, as in the latter passage, Jesus qualifies it in a similar way, that is, with a promise of the appearance of the Son of man. The high priest's reaction is immediate: Jesus is condemned of blasphemy.

The reader is in a unique position to judge all this. God himself has twice declared Jesus to be his Son (3:17; 17:5) and the Scriptures have verified it in a variety of ways. The council not only condemns him, they also abuse him physically and mock him, thereby mocking the Father who sent him. They even mock the Scriptures, asking him to prophesy (26:68), which, of course, he has done repeatedly. Now, however, their malice is clear. Thus the narrator depicts the opponents as insensitive leaders who mock their own religious tradition.

The disciples are not portrayed in much better light. Peter, the only one who has apparently not run away (26:69–75), is now said to be sitting in the courtyard. The narrator says Peter twice denied Jesus and the third time even cursed himself; his own words are quoted, doubling the effect of the denials. The assertion in 26:74 that he "began to invoke a curse on himself" demonstrates how far he has fallen. The incident ends with Peter weeping bitterly when he finally remembers Jesus' prediction. Thus, although Peter has refused to accept the persecution that Jesus suffers and predicted, he nevertheless returns to his senses and is filled with remorse: "He went out and wept bitterly" (26:75). This incident is another element in the narrator's complex portrait of the disciples.

The next phase of the persecution of Jesus takes place in the morning (27:1–2). The narrator merely reports the decision to condemn Jesus and his subsequent transfer to Pilate.

Before this second trial is described, the narrator intervenes to record the fate of Judas (27:3–10). We are told that he repented when he saw that Jesus was condemned; we must assume that Judas thought that the authorities would not be able to present a convincing case against him. The narrator does not explain Judas's motives, perhaps on purpose, simply reporting that Judas hanged himself. Thus the betrayer's death is described prior to the condemnation of Jesus. The thirty pieces of silver are invested in a field to be used as a cemetery for strangers. The unexpected element here is a fulfillment quotation (from Zech. 11:12–13 and Jer. 32:6–15) which clearly implies that what Judas has done is in no way beyond God's plans. Although he betrays Jesus, he cannot thwart what God has arranged. It is another subtle reminder to the reader of the primary focus of the story.

The narrator's emphasis in the confrontation between Jesus and

Pilate is the pressure that the Jewish authorities are able to put on Pilate. We have to fill in the gap of what the authorities have said to Pilate to justify their demand for his execution. Pilate's first question probably reflects the charges: "Are you the King of the Jews?" (27:11). Jesus' answer is the same as his answer before the high priest, without the reference to the Son of man (26:64). His continued silence in the face of further accusations leads the narrator to report that Pilate "wondered (marveled) greatly" (v. 14). This rare use of omniscience, ambiguous as it is, has the effect on the reader of placing Pilate in a more favorable light; he is amazed or perplexed. The word has been used by the narrator to describe the effect of miracles or the effect of an answer that is especially insightful.

The next paragraph (27:15–23) implies then that Pilate's offer to release Barabbas is a way of implementing his "wonder." But notice that it is the crowd that is offered the choice. And when the offer is made, the narrator *again* tells us Pilate's thoughts: "He knew it was out of envy that they had delivered him up" (v. 18). The ambiguity of the earlier statement is now gone: Pilate is suspicious of the authorities and the reader's sympathy is aroused. But that is not all. The very next sentence makes it clear that God himself continues to influence the action and, of course, on Jesus' behalf: Pilate's wife advises her husband to drop the whole issue because she "suffered much over him today in a dream" (v. 19). Dreams were clearly identified with revelation at the beginning of the story. And since Pilate's wife describes Jesus as "righteous," we are also reminded of the beginning of the story. Of course, it substantiates what we already know about Jesus.

Thus the juxtaposition of (1) a comment about Pilate's suspicions about the motives of the opponents with (2) the report of his wife's dream reinforces our image of Pilate and his attitude. When the next verse explains the reason for the people's attitude, that is, that they were persuaded by the chief priests and elders, the reader has been effectively encouraged to distrust the authorities. Pilate cannot get the crowd to give in to his wishes; the crowd demands crucifixion because they were pressured to do so.

So Pilate himself gives in, we are told, because he saw that a riot (27:24) was beginning (another instance of omniscience). He washes his hands, an empty gesture, which, however, affords the narrator the chance to report the people's curse upon themselves! Since the people seem to function as a voice for the elders in this scene, it is the elders who accept the responsibility and also refuse to answer Pilate's final, desperate question.

THE SON'S DEATH AND VINDICATION (27:27—28:20)

The Roman soldiers mock Jesus as a king and in the process inadvertently proclaim his true character (27:27–31). In their own way they associate themselves with the Sanhedrin who also mocked him.

The narrator's comment about Simon being compelled to carry the cross(27:32) implies both that Jesus could not shoulder it himself and that Simon might be a disciple (see 16:24). This is the only reference to him in the story.

The crucifixion is reported in a subordinate clause with an emphasis on the division of Jesus' garments by lot (27:35). The offered wine-gall mixture, which Jesus refuses, implies also that the gesture is not an act of mercy. Although the narrator does not mention any explicit OT predictions—the last formula quotation was in 27:9—the reader has been prepared throughout the story for OT references here at the climax. Their indirect use here is a further indication of the importance of symbolic language (and its interpretation) which Jesus has stressed. The notice attached to the cross (27:37) helps to confirm that the indictment brought against Jesus was that he "claimed" to be a king. The irony is obvious to the reader.

After a mere mention of the two robbers, the narrator details some of the crowd's reaction (27:38–44). We are told that the passers-by deride him (the Greek word is "blaspheme"), shaking their heads. They quote the false testimony about rebuilding the temple and then taunt him with a phrase that is similar to Satan's words at the temptation. Jesus maintains his silence; the reader knows his status. Next, the narrator explicitly mentions the authorities: their taunt also reminds the reader of the opening of the book. They claim that he can save others but not himself, that is, Jesus is called "Jesus" *because* he will save his people (see 1:21). They expect God to act on his behalf, as indeed he will, but not as they anticipate. Finally, the robbers are also said to revile him.

The ironies are complex but relatively clear. The Son of God is mocked because he obeys the Father.

The Son's death is recorded in somber tones (27:45–50). Jesus' only quoted words are in Aramaic and constitute a direct appeal to

God. The OT overtones are thereby intensified. The taunting of the crowd continues, trying to prolong his agony by offering him liquid to delay his death—to see if "Elijah" will indeed come. Jesus dies with a loud cry.

The significance of Jesus' death is stated in two ways: (1) with miraculous events, and (2) with the response of the centurion and those who were with him (27:51–54). It is not clear just which curtain of the temple is torn but the image of tearing implies both the idea of remorse and the impact of his death for the very heart of Jewish religion. The earthquake, the opening of tombs, and the imminent resurrection underscore divine involvement. The narrator clarifies how the reader should understand all this by reporting the soldiers' statement of faith. There can be little doubt about the importance of the contrast between the soldiers, on the one hand, and the Jewish crowd on the other.

The significance of reporting the presence of the women is not clear (27:55–56). They were not mentioned earlier in the story, by name or as a group, and the reader would be inclined to think of them in contrast to the disciples. It does demonstrate that *not everyone* has run away even though they stand in the background.

Matt. 27:57 introduces another new figure, Joseph of Arimathea, who takes responsibility for the burial of Jesus. Some of the women are mentioned again in 27:61, emphasizing their faithfulness.

This phase of the story concludes with an incident on the next day (27:62–66). The final appearance of the Jewish opponents underscores their perversity. Although they quote Jesus correctly, it is to win Pilate's approval to guard the tomb. Pilate continues to distance himself from the whole event by telling them that they can do this themselves if they wish. The tomb is sealed and guarded.

THE SON'S OBEDIENCE VINDICATED (28:1–20)

The conclusion of Matthew's story of Jesus comes as no surprise to the reader; we have been carefully prepared. Jesus' predictions have been accurate. The Father's control has been affirmed and demonstrated. The opponents have been portrayed in a consistent manner and their actions are understandable. Any uncertainty that remains in the mind of the reader will be, first, about the disciples and, second, about how the Father's will is to be accomplished.

Furthermore, the reader has been prepared to expect a balanced and carefully composed conclusion. It has often been noted that the final paragraphs recall features of the opening paragraphs. For example, "the angel of the Lord" describes the Father's messenger in the infancy stories as well as here in the account of the resurrection. Jesus is called "Emmanuel—God with us" in the beginning (1:23) and at the end he tells his disciples: "I am with you to the end of the age" (28:20). The artistry of the narrator is apparent.

On Sunday, the women who return to the tomb are those who were present at the burial. The narrator tells us they came to "see the sepulchre" (28:1). The appearance of an angel (28:2) occasions another earthquake, as did the Son's death in 27:51. Although the guards are said to be thoroughly frightened, the reaction of the women is not even mentioned. It is the angel's message, however, that is of primary importance: he knows why they have come, sends them to tell the disciples what they have seen and to remind them that Jesus will meet them in Galilee. This is an indirect way of letting us know that the disciples have not left the city, even though they had run away (26:56) from the earlier danger. When Jesus himself meets the women, they worship him, taking hold of his feet (28:9). Jesus' own message is similar to that of the angel and again specifically mentions the disciples. In this way the narrator keeps our attention focused on the disciples and reinforces the fact that the Father is guiding these events, even though the resurrection itself is not described. The tomb was empty, God's messenger appeared and spoke to the women, and the risen Jesus is seen and touched by the women.

Our final glimpse of the opponents (28:11–15) reinforces our perception of them: they are now reported to have fallen to the level of bribing the guards. In fact, they are quoted as saying that they will accept the responsibility for the deception and will square it with Pilate, just as they had influenced the crowd, two days earlier, to accept the responsibility for Jesus' death (27:24–25).

The story ends (28:16–20) with the disciples back in Galilee, where the story began and where their careers as disciples began. The narrator stresses that these unpredictable followers did obey the risen Lord's message. When Jesus himself appears among them, the narrator says they "worshipped him" (28:17) just as the women did when they met him earlier (28:9) and as the disciples had earlier when Jesus walked on the water (14:22–27). But the narrator here adds the significant comment: "but some doubted" (28:17)! This phrase should be translated: "but they were uncertain" or "but they were of two minds." It indicates that at the end of the narrative the disciples act in a way consistent with the picture the narrator has already presented. Even when they are confronted by the risen Lord, they are uncertain. Their faith is strong but not absolute. It is under these conditions, then, that Jesus' last words are spoken (28:18–20). He is quoted as reaffirming the basic themes of the story and, in effect, reminding the reader of the primary issues the narrator has placed before us. The Son has been given all authority by the Father, both in heaven and on earth—the point that was especially prominent in 11:25–30. He has not been abandoned by the Father; the resurrection verifies that his actions have been in accord with the Father's will.

Second, the "authorized Son" commands the disciples to "make disciples of (or disciplize) all nations," both the Gentiles and the Jews. Thus the narrator, in reporting the Son's final words, focuses our attention once again on the disciples. They are asked to go out and create more people like themselves, despite their limitations. "To make disciples" requires two major activities: baptizing and teaching.

The command to baptize new converts is another direct reminder of the opening of the story, that is, to the activity of John the Baptist and the baptism of Jesus. There has been no mention of baptism since the opening chapters. In addition, the trinitarian terminology is unique to the story. Story gaps of this sort encourage the reader to supply information from the contemporary community.

The second command is to teach the things which Jesus taught, with the added emphasis that these people must be taught to "obey." Such an emphasis has often been part of the narrator's story and was a primary feature in the Sermon on the Mount. One need only remember the crucial parable of the two houses that concluded that sermon (7:24–27), or the importance of the actions of the righteous ones (from all nations) in the parable of the judgment that concluded the final speech of Jesus (25:31–46). In the last words of the story, the Son promises the disciples: "I am with you always, till the close of the age" (28:20). The reader knows, from the speech in chaps. 24—25, that the end is imminent but cannot be calculated. The disciples were told at that time to watch. Now the Son promises that he will not abandon them, as they watch *actively* by increasing the number of disciples. We know that God does not abandon his own Son, and the Son now states that he will not abandon his followers. The reader is thus encouraged to remain active while seeking to understand the message of the Son/teacher who died to save others and was raised to carry out the Father's will.

Matthew's story of Jesus is indeed an artistic creation that in many and varied ways has transmitted its message to its readers. As our understanding of its details grows, we can anticipate a continual challenge and growing appreciation of the narrator's intent.